by Seamus McEvoy

get your ideal job

JOB-SEEKING
SKILLS
WORKBOOK
For Students

Gill & Macmillan Ltd
Hume Avenue
Park West
Dublin 12
with associated companies throughout the world
www.gillmacmillan.ie

© Seamus McEvoy, 2008

978 07171 4367 2

Design by Dowling & Dowling Design Consultants Limited
Print origination for this edition by O'K Graphic Design, Dublin

The paper used in this book is made from the wood pulp of managed forests. For every tree felled, at least one tree is planted, thereby renewing natural resources.

Contents

PART 1

INTRODUCTION TO JOB SEEKING

What does the employer want?

The employer has a vacancy and they need someone to fill that vacancy. They will have identified in general terms what main skills and attributes the successful candidate for the job should have. The employer wants to find the best possible candidate for the job.

What does the job seeker want?

The job seeker wants a job. They must convince the employer that they are the best person for the job. While this may sound easy, it requires a lot of preparation. You will not only have to convince the employer that you have the skills and attributes required, but that you are better at them than any other candidate.

Your successful job search

You have a big task on your hands if you are to be successful in your job search activities. The most important thing is preparation, preparation, and more preparation. You must be prepared even before a vacancy comes up. This means having:

- your CV ready,
- practised filling out application forms,
- prepared for and completed some interviews.

Build up your experience

You must continually build up your experiences, skills and achievements so that you are constantly increasing your chances to successfully apply for vacancies that come up.

1

THE JOB-SEEKING PROCESS EXPLAINED STEP BY STEP

We will describe each step in the next few pages.

Employer has vacancy

Job seeker wants job

STEP 1
Job Advertised
Newspaper
Internet
Local Notices
Existing Staff Contacts

STEP 2
Applications Received
Letter
Email
Telephone
CV
Application Form

STEP 3
Applicants Short Listed

STEP 4
Short Listed
Applicants Interviewed

STEP 5
Job Offer to
Successful Candidate

STEP 1
Job Advertised

How employers advertise jobs

The employer will identify that they have a vacancy perhaps arising from staff leaving or expansion. They will list the duties of the post and have a general idea of the skills and qualifications that a suitable candidate will need in order to do the job properly. This is very important from the employer's viewpoint. The clearer the employer is about what they want the person to do, the better chance they have of getting a good candidate for the job.

The employer wants to advertise their vacancy to as many job seekers as possible. The cost of attracting potential employees is expensive and employers are constantly looking for the lowest cost ways to advertise vacancies.

There are a number of ways to promote a job vacancy to job seekers.

1. Job Advertisement
In local or national newspapers, on radio, on local notice boards, specialist publications, etc. This is the most common method.
Depending on the type of media used (local or national) the cost can vary from cheap to extremely expensive. In many cases, a small ad in a local or regional paper or radio station is enough, as there will be many candidates within that area to meet the employers' needs.

For senior or important positions, employers will spend a lot of money to ensure that they get as many suitable applications for the job as possible. The jobs pages of national papers are generally taken by large companies who have lots of vacancies or an individual job at a high level.

2. The Internet
The Internet is a popular method of advertising vacancies. Internet recruitment sites include basic notice board sites where the job seeker can only view vacancies. Other sites act as matching agencies between employers and candidates. They allow job seekers to submit an online application free of charge and they then charge employers to search the database of applications held on the site.

As well as commercial recruitment websites, there are many other sources of vacancy information on the Internet. Most professional organisations will have vacancy information on their websites. Local paper and radio websites will have a vacancy notice board and many companies have a vacancy page on their website.

3. Recruitment Agencies
Many employers subcontract to a recruitment agency. These agencies charge a fee, normally a percentage of the first year's salary of the post and will bring the process through the initial stages, usually up to the interview. For senior posts, employers sometimes use specialist recruitment agencies called executive search agencies (or head-hunters) to approach potential candidates on their behalf.

A recent trend is for the recruitment agency to recruit staff as their employees and then subcontract those people to an employer. This method is used by larger companies as it reduces the administration and other costs required to recruit and employ staff.

4. Government Agencies

Agencies such as FÁS actively promote vacancies across a variety of sectors while specialised agencies such as Cert advertise jobs in the industry they work with. Most third-level institutions advertise vacancies for their graduates. There are many local employment agencies which help local employers advertise their vacancies.

5. Existing Staff and Contacts

Sometimes employers will advertise to people who worked for them in the past or who are working with them at present. They advertise the job to existing staff because they might know people who may be interested in working for them. This method is regularly used for filling short-term employment requirements. In some cases, employers will advertise the job internally before advertising it to the general public.

6. Recruitment Fairs

These are popular in times of high employment or for specialised sectors. They offer employers an opportunity to meet a large number of candidates in a single location over a short period of time. They are used by employers to support their recruitment advertising and encourage as many potential candidates as possible to apply for the jobs available.

STEP 2
Applications Received

The application process

This is the first point of contact between the employer and the job seeker. It takes a number of different forms.

1. Application Forms

Many employers have standard application forms for all vacancies. This form allows the employer to collect the same information from all candidates in a layout that lets them compare candidates easily and make a quick decision. Employers like application forms because they control what information is to be included by the job seeker. Application forms are very popular with larger employers who receive a large number of applications for a small number of jobs.

Many employers now use online application forms where the applicant fills out the form on the Internet and emails it to the employer. This is very common with graduate level jobs and for large employers. Recruitment websites also use online application forms.

2. Curriculum Vitae

A CV is the traditional method used to apply for jobs. A CV is basically a history of the candidate's experience and qualifications to date. The information in it allows the employer to make an assessment about whether the candidate is suitable for the job in question.

The difference between an application form and the CV is that the information in a CV is fully in the control of the job seeker. While there are advantages to this, it can also be a disadvantage to the job seeker – why? The job seeker has to decide what is relevant and what is not - they have to interpret what the employer is looking for and then promote themselves to the employer in a clear and concise way. With an application form the employer is telling the applicant what is relevant and the layout is standard.

3. Covering Letters / Email

It is normal practice to submit a covering letter with an application form or CV. This letter (or email for electronic applications) is a summary of the job seeker's skills and suitability for the job in question. It introduces the job seeker to the employer with the CV or application form giving detailed information.

4. Telephone

In a small number of cases, employers ask you to contact them by phone. In some cases, this is to speed up the recruitment process and the telephone conversation is really a mini interview, which can then lead to a more formal interview or a job offer.

5. Straight to Interview

Sometimes employers will hold walk-in interviews or employment open days. They advertise the time and location extensively and anybody can 'drop in' to meet the employer. Usually, you fill in a short application form when you arrive and have a discussion with the employer's representative. If they feel that you are a suitable candidate, they may do a formal interview with you on that day or arrange an interview for a later date. This method is often used when an employer has a large number of vacancies or in areas where it is difficult to recruit staff.

6. Speculative Applications

Job hunters sometimes write to employers in the hope that they have a vacancy. This is a hit and miss approach as there is an outside chance that the employer will have a vacancy. It is useful to follow up this approach with a telephone call, but you must be well prepared for the telephone call and treat it as an interview. Employers will often hold your CV for a period of time in case any suitable vacancies do come up. However to be safe, if you hear about a vacancy in that company, contact them to make sure that your application is included for that vacancy.

STEP 3
Applicants Short-listed

Short-listing applicants

Once the employer has received a number of applications they will usually short-list to select the best candidates for the post. Short-listing involves going through all applications and comparing them against each other and the requirements for the job. The purpose is to review each applicant to decide if they are suitable to bring forward to the next step in the selection process. Candidates that are not suitable are rejected at this point. Basically the employer looks at each application and asks 'Is it worth my while interviewing this person?'.

A common process used by many employers is after quickly reading each application, they sort them into three groups:

✔ **YES Interview Group** – those who are strong candidates for the job. These applicants will progress to the next stage of the recruitment process.

? **MAYBE Interview Group** – those who may have the potential to do the job in question. If there are not enough suitable applicants for interview at the end of the short-listing, the employer will return to this group and short-list again from it.

✖ **NO Interview Group** – those who are not suitable for the post due to insufficient experience or skills displayed in their application or CV. Those applicants will be eliminated from the process at this point.

In many cases the employer will know how many candidates they need to interview in order fill the job. This can vary from five to eight interviewees per job depending on the quality of applicants. If the employer finds that they have more candidates to interview than they need, they will short-list again to identify the stronger candidates to interview for the post. Where they do not have enough candidates, to interview, they will look at the candidates in the MAYBE Interview list and review their applications to see if they are suitable for interview.

This stage highlights the importance of having a good application/CV submitted to the employer. An application/CV which highlights your skills and qualities and matches them to the job in question will encourage the employer to put *your* application in the YES Category.

Yes Interview   Maybe Interview   No Interview

More short-listing – tests etc.

In some cases the employer will conduct more short-listing activities before they call you to interview. This happens when there are a large number of applicants for a small number of jobs. Employers use tests to further assess short-listed candidates before bringing them to interview. These tests could be aptitude tests that measure the key skills necessary to be successful in the job, e.g. numerical skills in a bank.

STEP 4
Short-listed
Applicants Interviewed

Interviews

The final part of the recruitment process is generally an interview where the employer will meet the candidate to discuss their application and find out more about them. The employer will decide whether or not to give you the job on the basis of that discussion. In some cases, employers will ask people to attend a number of interviews before they make a final decision. Each interview is effectively a short-listing exercise until they reach the final candidates.

The interview process can involve one person or a number of people (an interview panel) speaking to the candidate. An interview can take between 15 and 45 minutes depending on the employer and the job. During that time the job seeker has the opportunity to sell themselves to the employer and convince the employers that they are the best person for the job.

NOTE: **Sometimes employers use tests as a first method of short-listing, e.g. Gardai. They will ask all applicants to do the tests.**

STEP 5
Job Offer to
Successful Candidate

Got the job – Well done!

At this point, the employer will have made a decision to offer the job to the candidate, or candidates, who they feel are the most suitable. If you are the successful candidate, this is the end of this recruitment process for you.

Develop your skills and move your career forward

You should now use the opportunity to develop your skills and knowledge to move your career forward in the future. It is important that you continually look for opportunities to improve your job and salary over time. This may be with your new employer or with different employers in the future. Every job you have gives you an opportunity to learn new skills. By continually learning new things and combining them with your existing skills, you are improving your ability to compete for opportunities in the future.

Did not get the job – How to do better next time!

There will be candidates who are unsuccessful after going through all the stages of the job process. Don't be disheartened by failure to get a job. You will have learned from the exercise. Think about your performance and ask yourself how you can improve next time.

Areas to think about include:

1. Could you improve your performance in the recruitment process? Be honest with yourself, was your interview technique okay, did you get across all the relevant points etc. Identify areas where you need to improve your technique.

2. You may not have the required level of skills or other candidates had better skills for this job. The recruitment process helps you to identify skill gaps that you may have – think about what skill or experience gaps you have and find ways to fill these gaps so that you have a better chance for next time.

> *A job hunter's story can be described as no, no, no, no, no, no, no, YES! You only need to get one job to be successful, but you may apply for lots of jobs before you get that one job – don't give up, learn from each unsuccessful job hunt and continually improve your skills and attributes – you will get there eventually.*

Questions

List the methods used by employers to advertise jobs.
Which do you think is the best way?
Why do you think it is the best way?

Describe a common way that employers short-list candidates for a job vacancy.
If you were the employer, how would you short-list applicants?
What can a job seeker do to help them get through the short-listing process?

WHAT DO EMPLOYERS WANT?

The first question that the job seeker must answer is 'What is the employer looking for?' Employers' requirements vary from job to job and from company to company. Most employers will have a well-defined description of the job and type of person who would successfully fill the job.

Why employers employ staff?

When preparing to contact an employer, you must meet the employer's needs. To do this properly, you must understand why the employer is recruiting staff. An employer recruits staff as a means to an end. They are looking for somebody to whom they will pay a wage and in return will receive that person's labour. Employers are not charities and look at this from a commercial point of view.

'If it costs €10 per hour to employ you, will you generate more than €10 per hour benefit for my business?'

The benefit of employing staff can be judged by the value of better customer services, extra sales, savings in other areas etc. Employing people is a basic cost of running a business, the bottom line is that the employer needs to get more value from your work than they pay you in wages.

Things that employers look for in all employees.

Each employer and job will need different skills and qualities from the person doing the job. In some cases there are things that an employee must have, e.g. to work as an electrician you must be qualified.

There are other things that employers look for in their staff that will help the person do the job well.

Examples of general qualities that all employers look for:

(a) Motivation and enthusiasm – employers love people who are enthusiastic. Many employers say that if the applicant is enthusiastic, they can be taught the other parts of the job. Basic signs of the applicant's enthusiasm is the amount of effort that they took to find out about the company and the job and the effort they have put into their CV or application form.

(b) Teamwork – employers want people who can work as part of a team. Many companies are structured around a team where all members of the team are expected to contribute to the team. They need you, the applicant, to prove that you will work well as part of a team.

(c) Communication – both spoken and written. Again, this varies depending on the job in question. However, all jobs require communication skills in one form or other. You will have to talk to fellow employees, customers, suppliers and other people in your work. In order to do this you must be able to communicate clearly and effectively.

(d) Flexibility and adaptability – employers require people who are flexible and adaptable. They want people who are good at doing different tasks at different times or altogether. Employers need to be able to change very quickly and they want employees who can contribute to that.

(e) Problem solving and initiative – this is a basic requirement in all jobs. Employers want staff that are willing to make decisions and solve problems as they arise. They do not wish to have an employee who is running back to the supervisor looking for guidance all the time. They want somebody who can use their initiative and apply common sense so that a situation is resolved to the satisfaction of the employer and the customer.

WHAT ARE MY TRANSFERABLE SKILLS?

Skills are mentioned throughout this book – but what are skills? We often think of skills as things that we do in a work situation, e.g. using a piece of machinery/equipment, etc. However the most important skills for job seeking are those that we can use in many different situations. These are called transferable skills because you use them for different things and in different places, e.g. you learn to count in school, but use the skill in lots of situations outside school.

The following list describes some common transferable skills and examples of how we use them. Remember that you have many examples of using your skills. The skills and examples listed are a sample of the more common ones and is not a complete list.

Your transferable skills and examples of how you are using them now

Verbal communication skills

- Telling stories
- Explaining ideas to others
- Speaking in public
- Listening to others
- Finding words to describe things

Written communication skills

- Writing essays/stories/letters
- Reading
- Filling out forms

People skills

- Leading people
- Selling, persuading or influencing people
- Working in a team
- Sorting out disputes
- Listening to and helping others
- Teaching/training others
- Accepting criticism

Number skills

- Doing calculations
- Budgeting your money
- Remembering figures
- Estimating prices
- Show figures on a chart
- Working out averages, percentages etc.

Problem-solving skills

- Fixing things
- Understanding and interpreting information
- Working out travel routes
- Finding new ways to do things

Information technology skills

- Using computers and software packages such as spreadsheets, etc.
- Using mobile phones
- Using the Internet
- Fixing computers

Manual skills

- Keeping fit and involved in sports
- Operating machinery
- Dismantling or assembling things

Project management skills

- Organising events
- Following and giving instructions
- Planning activities
- Organising your study time

Learning skills

- Understanding how things work
- Learning new languages
- Understanding concepts

Creative skills

- Drawing and art
- Making artistic items
- Designing things
- Playing or composing music
- Involvement in drama

Understanding job advertisements

The job seeker must understand what the employer is looking for. If you understand the employer's needs, it is easier to write an application/CV that is aimed at meeting those needs. You can talk about your skills using the employer's language in an interview.

When employers are writing job advertisements, they try to explain what they require for the job. This lets applicants see if they have the skills and qualities necessary for that job. Job advertisements usually describe:

- Duties of the job – what work the job holder will be required to do.
- Specialist skills or qualifications necessary for the job, e.g. technical qualifications.
- General abilities that they would like candidates to have.
- What past experience is required.

Worksheet	Understanding job advertisements

Most newspapers will have a dedicated job section. The Irish Independent *on Thursdays, and the* Irish Times *and* The Examiner *on Fridays. Sunday newspapers have job supplements that are generally smaller than the daily papers. Regional and provincial newspapers will have jobs sections listing local jobs.*

From any of the newspapers mentioned, pick out three jobs with a detailed job description. Read them carefully and complete the following worksheet. They don't have to be jobs that you are going for now, but may be jobs that you are interested in for the future.

When you have completed this exercise discuss it with your classmates to see if they have identified different skills or attributes required.

NOTE: **As an additional exercise, you can use the Internet to find interesting job descriptions and complete the same exercise.**

	NAME OF JOB 1:	
	COMPANY NAME 1:	
What are the main duties of the job?		
What are the main skills required?		
What other skills or qualifications is the employer looking for?		
Any other relevant information?		
Where can you get extra information about the job?		
How to apply?		Closing Date:

NAME OF JOB 2:		
COMPANY NAME 2:		
What are the main duties of the job?		
What are the main skills required?		
What other skills or qualifications is the employer looking for?		
Any other relevant information?		
Where can you get extra information about the job?		
How to apply?		**Closing Date:**

NAME OF JOB 3:		
COMPANY NAME 3:		
What are the main duties of the job?		
What are the main skills required?		
What other skills or qualifications is the employer looking for?		
Any other relevant information?		
Where can you get extra information about the job?		
How to apply?		**Closing Date:**

You are doing a two-week work experience in a recruitment agency. Your boss has to write job advertisements for the list of jobs in the first column of the worksheet below. She has asked you to help her prepare the advertisements by listing the skills and qualifications required for each job. Fill in the boxes below with what you think an applicant would need to be successful in the jobs listed.

JOB TITLE	MAIN DUTIES	'MUST HAVE' SKILLS	OTHER SKILLS, QUALIFICATIONS OR EXPERIENCE REQUIRED
Nurse			
Garda			
Electrician			
Bank Employee			
Shop Employee			
Car Sales Person			
Vet			
Pop Star			
Artist			
Civil Servant			

PART 2

PREPARING FOR YOUR JOB-SEEKING ACTIVITIES

> **CONTENTS**
> **(i) Fail to prepare – prepare to fail**
> - What do you have to offer an employer?
> - Year diary
> - Weekly log sheets
> - Experience summary worksheets
>
> **(ii) The two S's of job hunting – substance and style**

FAIL TO PREPARE – PREPARE TO FAIL

This applies to many things in life such as study, sport and looking for a job.

Most people start their job-seeking activities with very little preparation beforehand. They immediately launch into writing their CV, a letter to an employer or application form without asking themselves:

✔ What information should I put into the application?
✔ What is the employer looking for?
✔ What strengths have I got over other applicants for the job?

This can lead to disaster. If you are not prepared, you will:

✘ produce a bad CV that does not represent you in the best light to an employer,
✘ write a long and garbled covering letter that does not relate to the job or alternatively, a short two-line letter that tells the employer nothing about you,
✘ do a bad interview where it is obvious to the interviewer that you have not thought about the job and what you can offer it.

Later in this book, we describe the job-seeking process in detail. A step-by-step approach is used for each element so that you can successfully prepare for your job hunt in an easy and organised way. For every activity, the first step is always the same.

Step 1. Prepare

In the job-seeking process, preparation means two things:

1. Knowing about the job and what the employer wants.

2. Knowing what you have to offer the job and employer.

We have covered what you need to know about the job and what the employer wants in Part 1 – Introduction to job seeking. This part will help **you** clearly describe what **you** have to offer the job and employer.

What do you have to offer an employer?

This is the basic question you must answer when you are trying to get a job.

The employer wants a person with certain skills and abilities to do a job for them. While you may know that you have the required skills, you must prove this to the employer. You do this by giving information and facts about yourself to the employer.

You must tell the employer:
- what you have done in the past,
- what you have achieved as a result of these activities,
- how it is relevant to the job that you are applying for now.

To do this properly, you need to think about what you have done so far and make those activities relevant to employers.

Job-seeking experience headings

Generally most experiences fall into one of the following job-seeking experience categories:

- School experience.
- Work experience.
- Extra-curricular/other experience.

These are the main headings you use when you are writing your CV or filling out an application form. This section of the book is designed to help you describe and record past experiences, and start recording new experiences in a way that will be easy to transfer to your CV or job application. It will also help you to prepare for future job interviews.

This is the hardest part of the job-seeking process. *WHY?* We have an awful lot of information about ourselves in our heads, but transferring that information onto paper or talking to other people about it can be difficult.

Help – I have no experience!!

If this is your first reaction to the comments on this page – don't panic. Believe it or not, you have lots of different types of experiences. During the past few years, you may have been involved in activities such as sport, voluntary and paid work, helping out at home, and of course, school activities. Your experiences are just limited from a job seeker's perspective.

Building up your experiences and skills

We build up our experiences and achievements over time. This develops and improves skills that help us become more employable. Your experiences so far are mainly related to school and extra-curricular activities. The skills that you develop doing these activities are valuable to employers because if you can use them in a school situation, then you can also use them in the workplace.

Make an effort to get involved in different activities and build up your skills. Soon you will have a comprehensive list of skills and experiences to include in your CV or job application.

My experience diary and log book

Name: _____

School: _____

Tel. no: _____

Email address: _____

Date of birth: _____

Date that you started this diary: _____

Class: _____

Purpose of this diary and log book

You can use this diary and log book to record and summarise all the activities that you take part in throughout your senior years in school. The skills that you learn from those activities will help when you are writing out a CV or job application or preparing for a job interview.

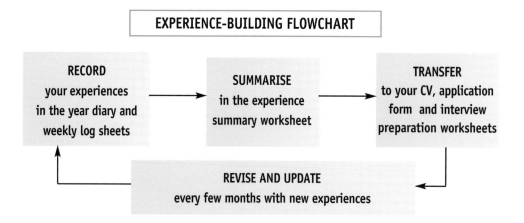

Filling out your experience diary and log book

1. Year diary   RECORD

This is a monthly diary for each year of your senior cycle. The year diary allows you to keep brief records of your experiences each month under each of the job-seeking experience headings.

● **School experience**

⇒ Exam results

⇒ School projects

⇒ Other academic activities or projects

⇒ Mini company responsibilities (this could also go under 'work experience')

⇒ School awards and scholarships

● **Work experience**

⇒ Part-time work during summer or at weekends

⇒ Work placements organised by your school

⇒ Work in family or related businesses

● **Extra-curricular/Other experience**

⇒ Sports activities

⇒ Community associations

⇒ Voluntary work (this could also go under 'work experience')

⇒ Adventure or activity weeks

⇒ Travel with your school or on holiday

2. Weekly log sheets   RECORD

These are weekly log sheets for detailed daily notes on work, community or other experiences that you may do as part of an organised placement. The weekly log is useful for transition year activities and organised work or community/social placements that you may do as part of your senior cycle curriculum.

3. Experience summary worksheets   SUMMARISE

These are designed to help you summarise and record relevant details of your experiences in a way that you can quickly transfer to your CV or job application. There is an experience summary worksheet for each experience heading – school, work and other. You just transfer the relevant information from your yearly diary or weekly log sheets. You should update your summary worksheet every few months.

My Transition Year Diary

Date	BRIEF DESCRIPTION OF YOUR EXPERIENCE/ACTIVITY		
	SCHOOL Include things that you have done during transition year including results in subjects, projects, essays etc.	**WORK** Include things you have done at work. If you work in a family business or farm include that as well.	**EXTRA CURRICULAR** Other activities that you may be involved with, e.g. sports clubs, voluntary associations etc.
Summer 20 —	**MY JUNIOR CERT RESULTS** Subject / Result		
September WEEK 1			
WEEK 2			
WEEK 3			
WEEK 4			
WEEK 5			
October WEEK 1			
WEEK 2			
WEEK 3			
WEEK 4			

My Transition Year Diary

Date		BRIEF DESCRIPTION OF YOUR EXPERIENCE/ACTIVITY		
		SCHOOL	**WORK**	**EXTRA CURRICULAR**
October	week 5			
November	WEEK 1			
	WEEK 2			
	WEEK 3			
	WEEK 4			
	WEEK 5			
December	WEEK 1			
	WEEK 2			
	WEEK 3			
	WEEK 4			
	WEEK 5			
January	WEEK 1			
	WEEK 2			
	WEEK 3			

Date		BRIEF DESCRIPTION OF YOUR EXPERIENCE/ACTIVITY		
		SCHOOL	WORK	EXTRA CURRICULAR
January	WEEK 4			
	WEEK 5			
February	WEEK 1			
	WEEK 2			
	WEEK 3			
	WEEK 4			
March	WEEK 1			
	WEEK 2			
	WEEK 3			
	WEEK 4			
	WEEK 5			
April	WEEK 1			
	WEEK 2			
	WEEK 3			

My Transition Year Diary

Date		BRIEF DESCRIPTION OF YOUR EXPERIENCE/ACTIVITY		
		SCHOOL	WORK	EXTRA CURRICULAR
April	WEEK 4			
	WEEK 5			
May	WEEK 1			
	WEEK 2			
	WEEK 3			
	WEEK 4			
	WEEK 5			
June	WEEK 1			
	WEEK 2			
	WEEK 3			
	WEEK 4			
	WEEK 5			

My Fifth Year Diary

Date	BRIEF DESCRIPTION OF YOUR EXPERIENCE/ACTIVITY		
	SCHOOL Include things that you have done during the year including results in subjects, projects, essays etc.	**WORK** Include things you have done at work. If you work in a family business or farm include that as well.	**EXTRA CURRICULAR** Other activities that you may be involved with, e.g. sports clubs, voluntary associations etc.
Summer 20 __			
September			
October			
November			
December			

My Fifth Year Diary

Date	BRIEF DESCRIPTION OF YOUR EXPERIENCE/ACTIVITY		
	SCHOOL	WORK	EXTRA CURRICULAR
January			
February			
March			
April			
May			
June			

My Sixth Year Diary

Date	BRIEF DESCRIPTION OF YOUR EXPERIENCE/ACTIVITY		
	SCHOOL Include things that you have done during the year including results in subjects, projects, essays etc.	**WORK** Include things you have done at work. If you work in a family business or farm include that as well.	**EXTRA CURRICULAR** Other activities that you may be involved with, e.g. sports clubs, voluntary associations etc.
Summer 20 __			
September			
October			
November			
December			

My Sixth Year Diary

Date	BRIEF DESCRIPTION OF YOUR EXPERIENCE/ACTIVITY		
	SCHOOL	**WORK**	**EXTRA CURRICULAR**
January			
February			
March			
April			
May			
June			

Weekly log sheets

The next part of your experience diary is weekly log sheets for detailed notes on work, community and other organised placements that you may do as part of your senior cycle. The log sheet is designed to help you record all the things that you did during the placement and to identify the skills that you developed during the week. Fill out the log sheet every day during the placement.

EXPERIENCE-BUILDING FLOWCHART

RECORD
your experiences
in the year diary and
weekly log sheets

→

SUMMARISE
in the experience
summary worksheet

→

TRANSFER
to your CV, application
form and interview
preparation worksheets

REVISE AND UPDATE
every few months with new experiences

EXPERIENCE ONE

Type of Placement   Work Experience ❑   Community/Social ❑   Other ❑ *Describe*_____

Experience Details

Dates: from   /   /   to   /   /   School contact person: _____Tel: _____

Name of employer/sponsor:_____Tel: _____

Address:_____

Contact/supervisor name:_____Tel:_____Fax:_____Email: _____

Describe main activity of employer/sponsor:_____

Pre-experience preparation

Start time: _____ Finish time: _____

Transport organised? (yes/no) _____

Transport details _____

_____

What is appropriate clothing for the placement? _____

_____

Lunch arrangements _____

Do you need to bring any documentation on the first day?

_____

_____

Describe what activities do you expect to be doing during this placement _____

_____

What do you hope to learn from this placement?_____

_____

_____

Health and Safety

Describe any health and safety precautions that are necessary for this placement _____

_____

Is protective clothing required?_____

Daily Diary [day 1]

Did you arrive on time? _____

Describe your jobs and activities today

Morning: _____

_____

_____

_____

_____

Lunchtime: _____

Afternoon: _____

_____

_____

_____

_____

How do you feel you got on today? _____

_____

_____

ABOUT MY FIRST DAY

Who did you meet when you arrived?_____

_____

_____

What responsibilities were you given? _____

_____

_____

Who did you work with today? _____

_____

_____

What was the best thing about the first day? ____ ____

_____

_____

What was the worst thing? _____

_____

_____

Daily Diary (day 2)

Describe your jobs and activities today

Morning. _____

_____

_____

_____

_____

Lunchtime: _____

Afternoon: _____

_____

_____

_____

Was today easier than yesterday? _____

Explain your answer _____

_____

_____

_____

Daily Diary (day 3)

Describe your jobs and activities today

Morning: _____

_____

_____

_____

_____

Lunchtime: _____

Afternoon: _____

_____

_____

_____

_____

General thoughts about today _____

_____

_____

_____

_____

ABOUT MY WORKPLACE

Describe the area/working conditions that you work in _____

_____

_____

What extra information do you now know about the organisation?

_____

_____

_____

What products or services does it provide? _____

_____

_____

How many people work there? _____

_____

Any other useful information about the organisation _____

_____

_____

_____

_____

THE PEOPLE I WORK WITH

Who do you work with and what are their jobs?_____

_____

_____

_____

What skills do they need to do their job? _____

_____

What training or qualifications do they need? _____

_____

How are you getting on with them? _____

_____

What have you done to get to know them? _____

_____

_____

What have you learned about working with other people so far this week?_____

_____

_____

Daily Diary [day 4]

Describe your jobs and activities today

Morning: _____

_____

_____

_____

_____

Lunchtime: _____

Afternoon: _____

_____

_____

_____

_____

Would you like this work as a career? _____

Explain your answer _____

_____

_____

WORK RULES

Name the main rules in the organisation _____

_____

_____

How is workers' timekeeping checked? _____

_____

What health and safety precautions are in place? _____

_____

What are the hygiene rules? _____

_____

What are the evacuation rules in case of emergency? _____

_____

What happens if a worker breaks the rules? _____

_____

Daily Diary [day 5]

Did you arrive on time? _____

Describe your jobs and activities today

Morning: _____

_____

_____

_____

Lunchtime: _____

Afternoon: _____

_____

_____

General thoughts about the week _____

_____

_____

_____

THE END OF THE WEEK

Was the experience different than you expected and in what way?

_____

_____

_____

_____

_____

What are the differences between this experience and school?

_____

_____

_____

_____

How do you feel you progressed in the week? _____

_____

_____

_____

_____

_____

Post-experience summary

Before you start this section have a quick look at your answers to the pre-experience and daily diary sections of this log sheet.

What did you learn from the experience? _____

_____

_____

_____

_____

_____

_____

What was the most enjoyable part of the experience and why?

_____

_____

_____

_____

What was the most difficult part of the experience and why?

_____

_____

_____

_____

How will this experience influence you in the future?

_____

_____

_____

What skills or personal qualities did you learn or improve

Name of skill/quality	Explain how you learned or improved this skill/quality

Employer/sponsor evaluation   *(Please rate the student under the following headings)*

	Rating Very Good, Good, or Needs Improvement	Advice to the student on how to improve or develop this area
Timekeeping		
Working with people		
Following instructions		
Using initiative		
Attitude		
Ability to learn new things		

Student signature _____

Employer/sponsor signature _____   Teacher signature _____

Type of Placement   Work Experience ❑   Community/Social ❑   Other ❑ *Describe* _____

Experience Details

Dates: from   /   /   to   /   /   School contact person: _____Tel: _____

Name of employer/sponsor: _____Tel: _____

Address:_____

Contact/supervisor name:_____ Tel: _____ Fax: _____ Email: _____

Describe main activity of employer/sponsor: _____

Pre-experience preparation

Start time:_____Finish time:_____

Transport organised? (yes/no) _____

Transport details _____

_____

What is appropriate clothing for the placement? _____

_____

Lunch arrangements _____

Do you need to bring any documentation on the first day?

_____

_____

Describe what activities do you expect to be doing during this placement _____

_____

What do you hope to learn from this placement? _____

_____

_____

Health and Safety

Describe any health and safety precautions that are necessary for this placement _____

_____

Is protective clothing required?_____

Did you arrive on time? _____

Describe your jobs and activities today

Morning: _____

_____

_____

_____

_____

Lunchtime: _____

Afternoon: _____

_____

_____

_____

_____

How do you feel you got on today? _____

_____

_____

ABOUT MY FIRST DAY

Who did you meet when you arrived?_____

_____

_____

What responsibilities were you given? _____

_____

_____

Who did you work with today? _____

_____

_____

What was the best thing about the first day? _____

_____

_____

What was the worst thing? _____

_____

_____

Daily Diary [day 2]

Describe your jobs and activities today

Morning: _____

_____

_____

_____

_____

Lunchtime: _____

Afternoon: _____

_____

_____

_____

Was today easier than yesterday? _____

Explain your answer _____

_____

_____

_____

ABOUT MY WORKPLACE

Describe the area/working conditions that you work in? _____

_____

What extra information do you now know about the organisation?

_____

_____

_____

What products or services does it provide? _____

_____

How many people work here? _____

Any other useful information about the organisation _____

_____

_____

_____

_____

Daily Diary [day 3]

Describe your jobs and activities today

Morning: _____

_____

_____

_____

_____

Lunchtime: _____

Afternoon: _____

_____

_____

_____

_____

_____

General thoughts about today _____

_____

_____

_____

THE PEOPLE I WORK WITH

Who do you work with and what are their jobs? _____

_____

_____

_____

What skills do they need to do their job? _____

_____

What training or qualifications do they need? _____

_____

How are you getting on with them? _____

_____

What have you done to get to know them? _____

_____

What have you learned about working with other people so far this week? _____

_____

_____

31

Daily Diary [day 4]

Describe your jobs and activities today

Morning: _____

_____

_____

_____

_____

Lunchtime: _____

Afternoon: _____

_____

_____

_____

_____

Would you like this work as a career? _____

Explain your answer _____

_____

_____

WORK RULES

Name the main rules in the organisation _____

_____

_____

_____

How is workers' timekeeping checked? _____

_____

What health and safety precautions are in place? _____

_____

What are the hygiene rules? _____

_____

What are the evacuation rules in case of emergency? _____

_____

What happens if a worker breaks the rules? _____

_____

Daily Diary [day 5]

Did you arrive on time? _____

Describe your jobs and activities today

Morning: _____

_____

_____

_____

Lunchtime: _____

Afternoon: _____

_____

_____

_____

General thoughts about the week _____

_____

_____

_____

THE END OF THE WEEK

Was the experience different than you expected and in what way? _____

_____

_____

_____

What are the differences between this experience and school?

_____

_____

_____

_____

How do you feel you progressed in the week? _____

_____

_____

_____

_____

Post-experience summary

Before you start this section have a quick look at your answers to the pre-experience and daily diary sections of this log sheet.

What did you learn from the experience? _____

_____

_____

_____

_____

_____

What was the most enjoyable part of the experience and why?

_____

_____

_____

What was the most difficult part of the experience and why?

_____

_____

_____

_____

How will this experience influence you in the future?

_____

_____

What skills or personal qualities did you learn or improve

Name of skill/quality	Explain how you learned or improved this skill/quality

Employer/sponsor evaluation *(Please rate the student under the following headings)*

	Rating Very Good, Good, or Needs Improvement	Advice to the student on how to improve or develop this area
Timekeeping		
Working with people		
Following instructions		
Using initiative		
Attitude		
Ability to learn new things		

Student signature _____

Employer/sponsor signature _____   Teacher signature _____

EXPERIENCE THREE

Type of Placement   Work Experience ❏   Community/Social ❏   Other ❏ *Describe* _____

Experience Details

Dates: from   /   /   to   /   /   School contact person: _____Tel: _____
Name of employer/sponsor: _____Tel: _____
Address:_____
Contact/supervisor name: _____ Tel: _____ Fax: _____ Email: _____
Describe main activity of employer/sponsor: _____

Pre-experience preparation

Start time: _____ Finish time: _____
Transport organised? (yes/no) _____
Transport details _____

_____

What is appropriate clothing for the placement? _____
_____
Lunch arrangements _____
Do you need to bring any documentation on the first day?

_____
_____

Describe what activities you expect to be doing during this placement _____

_____

What do you hope to learn from this placement?_____
_____
_____

Health and Safety

Describe any health and safety precautions that are necessary for this placement?_____
_____

Is protective clothing required?_____

Daily Diary [day 1]

Did you arrive on time?_____

Describe your jobs and activities today
Morning: _____
_____
_____
_____
_____
_____

Lunchtime: _____

Afternoon: _____
_____
_____
_____
_____

How do you feel you got on today? _____
_____
_____

ABOUT MY FIRST DAY
Who did you meet when you arrived?_____
_____
_____

What responsibilities were you given? _____
_____
_____

Who did you work with today? _____
_____
_____

What was the best thing about the first day? _____
_____
_____

What was the worst thing? _____
_____

Daily Diary [day 2]

Describe your jobs and activities today

Morning: _____

_____

_____

_____

_____

Lunchtime: _____

Afternoon: _____

_____

_____

_____

Was today easier than yesterday? _____

Explain your answer _____

_____

_____

_____

Daily Diary [day 3]

Describe your jobs and activities today

Morning: _____

_____

_____

_____

Lunchtime: _____

Afternoon: _____

_____

_____

_____

_____

General thoughts about today _____

_____

_____

_____

ABOUT MY WORKPLACE

Describe the area/working conditions that you work in _____

_____

What extra information do you now know about the organisation?

_____

_____

_____

What products or services does it provide? _____

_____

How many people work there? _____

Any other useful information about the organisation _____

_____

_____

_____

_____

THE PEOPLE I WORK WITH

Who do you work with and what are their jobs?_____

_____

_____

What skills do they need to do their job? _____

_____

What training or qualifications do they need? _____

_____

How are you getting on with them? _____

What have you done to get to know them? _____

_____

What have you learned about working with other people so far this week?_____

_____

_____

Daily Diary [day 4]

Describe your jobs and activities today

Morning: _____

_____

_____

_____

Lunchtime: _____

Afternoon: _____

_____

_____

_____

Would you like this work as a career? _____

Explain your answer _____

_____

_____

WORK RULES

Name the main rules in the organisation _____

_____

_____

_____

How is workers' timekeeping checked? _____

_____

What health and safety precautions are in place? _____

_____

What are the hygiene rules? _____

_____

What are the evacuation rules in case of emergency? _____

_____

What happens if a worker breaks the rules? _____

_____

Daily Diary [day 5]

Did you arrive on time? _____

Describe your jobs and activities today

Morning: _____

_____

_____

_____

Lunchtime: _____

Afternoon: _____

_____

_____

_____

General thoughts about the week _____

_____

_____

THE END OF THE WEEK

Was the experience different than you expected and in what way? _____

_____

_____

_____

What are the differences between this experience and school? _____

_____

_____

_____

How do you feel you progressed in the week? _____

_____

_____

_____

Post-experience summary

Before you start this section have a quick look at your answers to the pre-experience and daily diary sections of this log sheet.

What did you learn from the experience? _____

_____

_____

_____

_____

_____

What was the most enjoyable part of the experience and why?

_____

_____

_____

What was the most difficult part of the experience and why?

_____

_____

_____

_____

How will this experience influence you in the future?

_____

_____

What skills or personal qualities did you learn or improve?

Name of skill/quality	Explain how you learned or improved this skill/quality

Employer/sponsor evaluation *(Please rate the student under the following headings)*

	Rating Very Good, Good, or Needs Improvement	Advice to the student on how to improve or develop this area
Timekeeping		
Working with people		
Following instructions		
Using initiative		
Attitude		
Ability to learn new things		

Student signature _____

Employer/sponsor signature _____ *Teacher signature* _____

EXPERIENCE FOUR

Type of Placement Work Experience ❏ Community/Social ❏ Other ❏ *Describe* _____

Experience Details

Dates: from / / to / / School contact person: _____Tel: _____
Name of employer/sponsor:_____ Tel: _____
Address:_____
Contact/supervisor name: _____ Tel: _____ Fax: _____ Email: _____
Describe main activity of employer/sponsor:_____

Pre-experience preparation

Start time: _____ Finish time: _____
Transport organised? (yes/no) _____
Transport details _____
_____
What is appropriate clothing for the placement? _____
_____
Lunch arrangements _____
Do you need to bring any documentation on the first day?
_____
_____

Describe what activities you expect to be doing during this placement _____
_____

What do you hope to learn from this placement? _____
_____
_____

Health and Safety

Describe any health and safety precautions that are necessary for this placement?_____
_____

Is protective clothing required?_____

Daily Diary (day 1)

Did you arrive on time? _____

Describe your jobs and activities today
Morning: _____
_____
_____
_____
_____

Lunchtime: _____

Afternoon: _____
_____
_____
_____
_____

How do you feel you got on today? _____
_____
_____

ABOUT MY FIRST DAY
Who did you meet when you arrived?_____
_____
_____

What responsibilities were you given? _____
_____
_____

Who did you work with today? _____
_____
_____

What was the best thing about the first day? _____
_____
_____

What was the worst thing? _____
_____
_____

Daily Diary [day 2]

Describe your jobs and activities today

Morning: _____

_____

_____

_____

_____

Lunchtime: _____

Afternoon: _____

_____

_____

_____

Was today easier than yesterday? _____

Explain your answer? _____

_____

_____

_____

ABOUT MY WORKPLACE

Describe the area/working conditions that you work in? _____

_____

_____

What extra information do you now know about the organisation?

_____

_____

_____

What products or services does it provide? _____

_____

_____

How many people work there? _____

_____

Any other useful information about the organisation _____

_____

_____

_____

_____

Daily Diary [day 3]

Describe your jobs and activities today

Morning: _____

_____

_____

_____

_____

Lunchtime: _____

Afternoon: _____

_____

_____

_____

_____

_____

General thoughts about today _____

_____

_____

_____

THE PEOPLE I WORK WITH

Who do you work with and what are their jobs?_____

_____

_____

_____

What skills do they need to do their job? _____

_____

_____

What training or qualifications do they need? _____

_____

_____

How are you getting on with them? _____

_____

What have you done to get to know them? _____

_____

_____

What have you learned about working with other people so far this week ? _____

_____

_____

39

Daily Diary [day 4]

Describe your jobs and activities today

Morning: _____

_____

_____

_____

_____

Lunchtime: _____

Afternoon: _____

_____

_____

_____

_____

Would you like this work as a career? _____

Explain your answer _____

_____

_____

Daily Diary [day 5]

Did you arrive on time? _____

Describe your jobs and activities today

Morning: _____

_____

_____

_____

_____

Lunchtime: _____

Afternoon: _____

_____

_____

_____

General thoughts about the week _____

_____

_____

_____

WORK RULES

Name the main rules in the organisation _____

_____

_____

How is workers' timekeeping checked? _____

_____

What health and safety precautions are in place? _____

_____

What are the hygiene rules? _____

_____

What are the evacuation rules in case of emergency? _____

_____

What happens if a worker breaks the rules? _____

_____

THE END OF THE WEEK

Was the experience different than you expected and in what way? _____

_____

_____

_____

What are the differences between this experience and school?

_____

_____

_____

_____

How do you feel you progressed in the week? _____

_____

_____

_____

_____

Post-experience summary

Before you start this section have a quick look at your answers to the pre-experience and daily diary sections of this log sheet.

What did you learn from the experience? _____

_____

_____

_____

_____

_____

_____

What was the most enjoyable part of the experience and why?

_____

_____

_____

_____

What was the most difficult part of the experience and why?

_____

_____

_____

_____

How will this experience influence you in the future? _____

_____

_____

What skills or personal qualities did you learn or improve?

Name of skill/quality	Explain how you learned or improved this skill/quality

Employer/sponsor evaluation *(Please rate the student under the following headings)*

	Rating Very Good, Good, or Needs Improvement	Advice to the student on how to improve or develop this area
Timekeeping		
Working with people		
Following instructions		
Using initiative		
Attitude		
Ability to learn new things		

Student signature _____

Employer/sponsor signature _____ Teacher signature _____

Experience summary worksheet

In the first two parts of your diary and log book, you have recorded details of your year's experiences. The experience summary worksheets are designed to help you summarise the relevant details of your experiences in a way that you can quickly transfer to your CV or job application. There is an experience summary worksheet for each experience heading – school, work and other. Update each worksheet every few months.

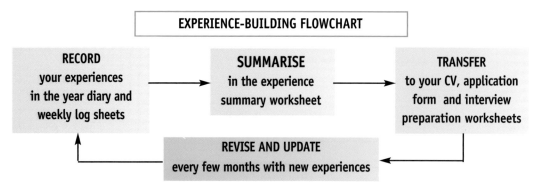

How to complete your experience summary sheets

COLUMN 1 – **BRIEF DESCRIPTION OF THE ACTIVITY**

Transfer brief details of the experience from year diary or log book into the relevant worksheet.

COLUMN 2 – **MY RESPONSIBILITIES / DUTIES**

List the responsibilities and duties that you had:

- Examples of responsibilities in work situations are if you were responsible for cash, dealing with customers, locking up or opening premises, training or supervising other staff, etc.
- Examples of extra-curricular responsibilities could include your position of responsibility within a club or team.

COLUMN 3 – **EXAMPLES OF MY ACHIEVEMENTS IN THIS ACTIVITY**

Your successes and achievements provide proof of your ability to complete the task or activity described, for example:

- success in a competition – sports or otherwise,
- sales, production, and other results in a transition year mini company,
- exam or projected results and grades,
- numbers of customers served, average transactions successfully completed whilst working as a cashier.

| REMEMBER | Where possible, state specific information that proves the point, e.g. raised €1,000 for a local charity sounds much better than raised a lot of money for charity. |

COLUMN 4 – **SKILL(S) LEARNED**

The purpose of this column is to get you to think about your experiences in terms of skills that you have learned. These may be technical skills such as using pieces of equipment or people skills such as communication etc. Don't worry if you are repeating a skill in a number of activities – this just shows that you have used that skill a number of times.

BLANK SPACES IN THE WORKSHEETS?

You may have lots of things to put into one sheet, but the others look blank. This gives you an indication of gaps in your CV and areas where you need to get some experience.

MY SCHOOL EXPERIENCE SUMMARY

Dates and a brief description of the activity	My responsibilities/actions	Examples and proof of my successes/ achievements in this activity	Skill(s) learned

HAVING DIFFICULTY? – Write an essay – If you find it hard to fill in the boxes, write out a short essay or story about your experience using the headings on the worksheet as the starting point of each paragraph, or section, of your story.

MY WORK EXPERIENCE SUMMARY

Dates and a brief description of the activity	My responsibilities/actions	Examples and proof of my successes/ achievements in this activity	Skill(s) learned

HAVING DIFFICULTY? – Write an essay – If you find it hard to fill in the boxes, write out a short essay or story about your experience using the headings on the worksheet as the starting point of each paragraph, or section, of your story.

MY EXTRA-CURRICULAR/OTHER EXPERIENCE SUMMARY

Dates and a brief description of the activity	My responsibilities/ actions	Examples and proof of my successes/ achievements in this activity	Skill(s) learned

HAVING DIFFICULTY? – Write an essay – If you find it hard to fill in the boxes, write out a short essay or story about your experience using the headings on the worksheet as the starting point of each paragraph, or section, of your story.

Tips

45

THE TWO S's OF JOB HUNTING – SUBSTANCE AND STYLE

When you are looking for a job, the two basic things that get an employer to seriously consider your application are:

SUBSTANCE

Information and facts about your skills, abilities and experiences that show your potential as an employee.

Your past activities and achievements are indicators of your future potential. Sports are an example of how this works. If you have been playing a sport for a few years and are now competing for a place on a team. The team manager will judge how you performed in the past and will use that information to decide if he/she will include you in the team. If you haven't been involved in the sport at all, it is harder for them to make the decision.

The same thing happens when an employer is looking at you. What you have achieved in the past is an indicator to the employer of your future potential. You must promote your achievements to help the employer decide positively for you.

FOR EXAMPLE
- Exam results are an indicator of your ability to concentrate and learn.
- Work experience is an indicator of your ability to get on with other people, with customers, with fellow employees.
- Activities in clubs, etc. indicate how you operate as a team player or display leadership and other qualities that an employer might be looking for.

All your experiences indicate to an employer how you might deal with situations that you could encounter in the workplace e.g. meet deadlines, solve problems, deal with customers etc.

STYLE

Every contact that you have with an employer must be professional and business-like.

In the same way that you will form an impression of somebody on your first meeting, (sometimes the wrong impression!) your contact with the employer creates an impression of you in the employer's mind.

You must create a positive impression right from the start. Your CV, application form, letter, telephone call, etc. must reflect you in a positive and professional manner.

PART 3

CONTACTING AN EMPLOYER

CONTENTS

(i) Your CV – the starting point of your job-seeking activities

- CVs – The employer's point of view
- Four-step process to a great CV
- Sample CVs
- CV editing worksheet
- How employers short-list CVs

(ii) Positive words to use for job seeking

(iii) Completing an application form

- Three-step process to completing an application form

- Application form practice worksheets
- Online applications and electronic short-listing

(iv) Writing a covering letter

- The function of a covering letter
- Writing a covering letter – the golden rules
- Three-step process to completing a covering letter

(v) Electronic applications

YOUR CV – THE STARTING POINT OF YOUR JOB-SEEKING ACTIVITIES

Writing your CV is the launch pad for applying for any job. Why? – because your CV is a list of all the things that you have to offer an employer. Completing a CV provides you with a basis for other job-seeking activities including application forms, covering letters, even contacting an employer by telephone.

How is a CV the basis for other job-seeking activities?

Writing or emailing an employer about a job opportunity – A covering letter or email is a summary of your skills and qualities. By completing the CV first, you identify your main strengths and can then write a covering letter that includes those strengths.

Completing an application form – The information on your CV is the same information that you put into an application form. When you start an application form, you pick the main points from your CV and transfer them to the relevant section of the application form.

Applying by telephone – When applying by telephone, you use your CV to help you talk about the main points that you want to make. If you have sent your CV to the employer before the telephone conversation, there is a good chance that they are looking at it while they are speaking to you.

In an interview – The employer will usually have your CV with them at an interview. If you bring a copy of it to the interview, you can use it to highlight successes to convince the employer that you are the right person for the job.

CVs – the employer's point of view

The employer is looking for a number of things from a CV.

Basic Information

An employer wants to know:
- who you are,
- where you're from,
- how they can contact you.

The best candidate for the job may not get an interview if they submit a poor CV, but a poor or average candidate who submits a good CV will get an interview.

However, the real question they are asking themselves is . . .

'Should I spend my valuable time interviewing this candidate?'

After looking at your CV, the employer has to decide if it is worth their while to interview you. You must convince them that you have the basic requirements for the job and more – that you are better than all the other candidates for the job. Employers are busy people and will not waste their time interviewing you for a job that they think you are unsuitable for.

CURRICULUM VITAE – Introduction

A CV has one job – **to get you a interview**. Sending your CV is the first contact with an employer. You may send it in response to an advertisement or it may be a speculative CV (which means that you are sending it in case they have a vacancy or will have one soon).

After reading your CV, the employer will decide whether it is worth their while interviewing you.

> ## The job of a CV – to get you an interview

4-Step Process to a Great CV

Step 1. **Prepare** all the relevant information that you need to put in your CV.

Step 2. **Write** a first draft with all the relevant information laid out in a basic CV structure.

Step 3. **Edit, edit and edit again,** fine tune the information and improve your layout a few times.

Step 4. **Revise and update** including new activities, achievements and responsibilities. Delete old items that may not be relevant anymore. You will constantly upgrade your CV throughout your career.

Step 1. Prepare

You have done this already. The experience summary worksheets that you completed in Part 2 are the preparation for your CV. In the next steps, you will use the information that you put into those worksheets to prepare a comprehensive CV. Move onto step 2.

Step 2. Write your CV

BEFORE YOU START WRITING, REMEMBER THE TWO S's OF JOB HUNTING

CV rules – SUBSTANCE

Positive items only. A CV is a positive document whose job is to get you an interview. Do not put anything into it that will give the interviewer a reason not to interview you!

Highlight your skills throughout the CV. Use every part of your CV as an opportunity to highlight your skills, qualities, experiences and achievements. A short personal career statement at the start of the CV that summarises your skills and qualities can be a good way to set the tone for the rest of your CV.

So what? If I was the employer, would I be impressed by this information? Always look at the CV from the employer's point of view since this is the person who is going to make a decision on the CV.

Relevant information only. Don't fill up your CV with irrelevant information. Build up relevant items to put into your CV by getting involved in clubs, getting work experience, improving exam results etc.

Accurate information only. Do not put false information in your CV. You will get caught out at interview – think about the unfortunate girl who stated that she was a fluent French speaker and ended up being interviewed by a French-speaking interviewer! Give an accurate description of your competency in something i.e. conversational French, written French, Leaving Cert French.

Do you include a photo with your CV? Generally no, but sometimes an employer will ask for a photograph. If you have to provide one, make sure that it is a good photograph not a cutout from a party, a family occasion or a debs!

CV rules – STYLE

Reverse chronological order. You are as good as your last game! Put work experience, education etc. in reverse order, i.e. the most recent item or activity first.

CVs should be typed. Hand-written CVs are not acceptable. A word-processed CV displays your ability to use a computer. Tips for word processing CVs are listed on page 58.

The generally accepted size of a CV is no more than two A4 pages. In the US, many employers prefer one page but the rule of thumb in Ireland is that it should be no longer than two A4 pages.

Use headlines. When you look at a daily paper or magazine, you glance at the headlines and then read the text. Your CV should also use headlines to highlight relevant information. Highlight key points using bold text to show the employer an area of relevance. On reading the headline they are then encouraged to read further into the content.

Exercise

Take yesterday's newspaper and pick three effective headlines that make you read further.

Use bullet points. Reading a long paragraph can be hard, whereas reading bullet points is easy. Keep to five or six bullet points for each heading. Bullet points should be one to two sentences in length. Bullet points support your headlines. You are making it easier for the employer to read your CV.

Use space effectively and avoid clutter. It is very hard to read something when the text is all over the place, very small or badly laid out. Ensure that the layout and look of your CV is balanced and that there are not big gaps or white spaces in your CV.

You are now at a point where you can start your CV properly. In the next pages there are sample CVs and a CV structure listing the information that you need to put into your CV.

Your CV must be clear, concise, and easy to read.

Sample 1

David O'Connor

Address: Ballinrostig, Gorey, Co Wexford
Telephone: 000 0000000
Email: davidoconnor@yahoo.com

Date of Birth: 5 September 1989

SKILLS PROFILE

- Excellent team-working ability
- Very good communication skills
- Ability to work well under pressure

EDUCATION

2001 – 2007
CBS, Gorey, Co Wexford

Leaving Certificate (2004):

Irish (H)	Accounting (H)
English (O)	Business Studies (H)
Mathematics (H)	Technical Drawing (H)
French (H)	

Junior Certificate (2001):

Irish	C (H)	French	C (H)
English	B (O)	Technical Graphics	A (H)
Mathematics	C (H)	Business Studies	B (H)
History	A (O)	Science	C (H)
Geography	B (H)	Civic, Social & Political Education	B

1993 – 2001
Scoil Iosagáin, Gorey, Co Wexford

EMPLOYMENT

June 2005 – Ongoing
Tesco, Gorey

- Full-time during holidays, Weekends during term-time
- Organising stock in storage areas
- Stocking shelves and price checking
- Dealing with customer queries

2001 – Ongoing Family Farm

- Tending to cattle including feeding calves and milking cows
- Driving tractor and spreading fertiliser in fields
- Assisting with vet visits (TB Testing, etc.)

I.T. SKILLS

Proficient user of Microsoft Word, the Internet and email.

INTERESTS & ACHIEVEMENTS

Member of Gorey GAA Club. Play both Hurling and Football. Captain of U16 football team, won County Final. Member of Gorey CBS Hurling Team, reached semi-final stage.

Member of local Athletics Club. As a middle distance athlete, I compete cross-country, road races, track and field events and relays. Won silver medal at All-Ireland Championship in 2005.

Awarded Transition Year Student of the Year. Participated in outdoor pursuits course, financial controller of mini-company.

School Prefect (Fifth Year): Attending School Council meetings, acting as spokesperson for class, ensuring safety of younger students during fire alarms.

Follower of Soccer (Manchester United) and Formula One.

Participate in the annual beach clean-up organised by the local Community Council on a voluntary basis.

Provisional Driving Licence.

REFERENCES

Mr John Murphy, Principal, Christian Brothers School, Gorey, Co Wexford. Tel: 000 0000000	Ms Nicola O'Brien, Manager, Tesco (Ireland) Ltd, Gorey, Co Wexford. Tel: 000 0000000

REMEMBER These are samples of very good CVs. Over time you should work to build up your experiences to have a comprehensive CV like these.

Address: Ballygaddy Road, Tuam, Co Galway
Telephone: 093 00000
Email: jenkelly@hotmail.com

JENNIFER KELLY

PROFILE
An innovative and reliable school leaver with excellent organisational skills and the ability to work well with others.

EDUCATION
2002 – Ongoing

St Colman's Community College,
Tuam,
Co Galway

Leaving Certificate Subjects:

Irish (L)	English (H)	German (L)
Music (H)	Chemistry (H)	Mathematics (H)
Physics (H)	Applied Maths (H)	

Junior Certificate Results (2005):

'A' Grade in Science (H) and Mathematics (H)
'B' Grade in Geography (H), Music (H), Irish (H), German (L)
'C' Grade in History (H), English (H) and Business (H)

1994-2002
Scoil Mhuire, Tuam, Co Galway

EMPLOYMENT
2006 – Ongoing

Leonardo's Bistro,
The Square,
Tuam,
Co Galway.

Waitress
• Greeting guests and seating them
• Taking orders and serving meals
• Dealing with queries and complaints
• Handling large amounts of money
• Providing a high level of customer service

Sample 2

EMPLOYMENT
2006

St Colman's Community College,
Tuam,
Co Galway

Exam Attendant
• Providing assistance to Exam Supervisor
• Worked as part of a team to organise and maintain the exam halls
• Assisted in distributing exam material and collected it after the exams

2004 – Ongoing

Various families
Babysitter/Childminder

INTERESTS
Gymnastics: Member of Tuam Gymnastics Club. Competed to All-Ireland Level. Assist with junior classes.

Music: Lead role in school musical 'Calamity Jane'. Member of school choir. Play violin (Grade 8).

Quizzes: Member of school quiz team. Finalists in Connaught School Quiz Competition.

Fundraising: Member of organising committee of sponsored walk in aid of Chernobyl Children's Fund. Raised €1950.

ADDITIONAL INFORMATION
Gaisce Presidents Award Scheme: Achieved Bronze Medal

Date of Birth: 3 February 1990

Driving Licence: Provisional

REFEREES

Ms Ciara O'Neill,	Ms Sinead Ryan,
Manager,	Principal,
Leonardo's Bistro,	St Colman's Community College,
The Square,	Tuam,
Tuam,	Co Galway.
Co Galway.	
Tel: 093 00000	Tel: 093 00000

Sample 3

Diane Roche

Ross Road, Killarney, Co Kerry
Tel: xxxxxxx, Email: diane_in_killarney@yahoo.com
Date of Birth: 24 June 1989

PROFILE

A professional individual with excellent interpersonal skills wishes to secure a position with a Travel Company for the summer before starting a course in Travel and Tourism in October. Ideal candidate for a position requiring drive, initiative and responsibility.

EDUCATION

St Mary's Presentation Secondary School, Killarney
2001 – 2007

Leaving Certificate (2005):

- Irish (H)
- Music (H)
- English (O)
- Business Studies (H)
- Mathematics (H)
- Geography (H)
- French (H)
- Art (H)

Junior Certificate (2002):

• Irish	C (H)	• French	A (H)
• English	B (O)	• Art	A (H)
• Mathematics	C (H)	• Business Studies	B (H)
• History	A (O)	• Science	C (H)
• Geography	B (H)	• Music	B (H)

1993 – 2001
Scoil Bríd, Killarney

EMPLOYMENT

Dunnes Stores, Killarney, Co Kerry

2005 – Ongoing

Sales Assistant
- Serving customers in grocery department.
- Handling large volumes of cash. This includes correct use of cash register and lotto machine and balancing cash intake at end of day.
- Stocking shelves and participating in regular stocktaking duties.
- Completed courses in Customer Care and Health and Safety in the Workplace.

Budget Travel, Killarney, Co Kerry

March 2005

Transition Year Work Experience (2 Weeks)
- Assisted at holiday desk.
- Prepared packs for postage.
- Filed clients information correctly.
- Taught how to check availability in Budget booking system.

POSITIONS OF RESPONSIBILITY

Assistant Manager of TSB School Bank Branch (2005): Responsible for ensuring that all money received was accounted for and lodged with the TSB.

Class Representative (2004): Responsibilities included acting as spokesperson for class, liaising with teachers, attending class council meetings, organising fundraising activities, organising Christmas party.

SKILLS

Organisational: Effective at managing time and prioritising tasks.

Communication and Interpersonal: Strong team-working and leadership skills.

Computer: Proficient user of Microsoft PowerPoint, Word and Excel, the Internet and email. Achieved honours in Department of Education Typing Examination.

Language: Good standard of French and Irish.

INTERESTS

Member of Killarney 'No Name' Club: Participate in wide range of activities including debating, sport, variety show, etc.

Volleyball: Currently member of senior school team.
Captain of junior school team that won Munster Final.
Completed refereeing course. Assist coaching younger teams.

ADDITIONAL INFORMATION

Provisional Driving Licence.

French: Moderate level of fluency. Achieved 'A' Grade in Junior Certificate. Participated in 2-week French Exchange in Transition Year. Returned to family for 2 weeks again last summer.

REFERENCES

Ms Fiona O'Hanlon,
HR Manager,
Dunnes Stores,
Killarney,
Co Kerry.
Tel: xxxxxxxx

Sr Anne O'Brien,
Principal,
St Mary's Presentation
Secondary School,
Killarney, Co Kerry.
Tel: xxxxxxx

Tómas Coleman

Address: 8 Castleshannon, Kells, Co Kildare
Tel: xxxxxxx, Email: tomcole@hotmail.com
Date of Birth: 5 December 1990

Sample 4

PERSONAL SKILLS/QUALITIES

- Good communication skills
- Customer service skills
- Flexible and wiling to learn
- Excellent organisational skills

EDUCATION

Secondary School
Kells Community College
2002 – 2007

Leaving Certificate Applied
Vocational Specialisms:
- Engineering
- Technology

Junior Certificate
- Technology (H)
- Technical Graphics (H)
- Metalwork (H)
- Business Studies (H)
- English (O)
- Science (O)
- Irish (H)
- Spanish (O)
- Mathematics (O)

Primary School
Kells NS
- Received a Certificate for Six Years Unbroken Attendance at School.

EMPLOYMENT

Xtravision, Kells, Co Kildare
June 2005 – Ongoing
Counter Assistant
- Checking out video/dvd rentals through system
- Accepting payment for rentals and sales
- Balancing till an end of night
- Checking returned videos/dvds
- Returning stock to shelves
- Maintaining and organising stock on shelves
- Ensuring general tidiness of premises

COMPUTER SKILLS

- Have experience of utilising HTML for creation of web pages.
- Regularly use Internet and Email.
- Proficient user of MS Word, Excel, PowerPoint and Access.
- Enjoy playing games on Playstation 2.

INTERESTS

Music:
- Play guitar in a band.
- Regularly work as DJ at local youth club.

Tae-Kwon Do:
- Member of the Kells Tae-Kwon Do Club.
- Granted the rank of Black Belt with the Tae Kwon-Do Federation of Ireland in 2003.

VOLUNTARY WORK

Frequently collect money on a voluntary basis for charities such as St Vincent de Paul and Chernobyl Children's Project.

Member of organising committee of a 10k walk in aid of the Chernobyl Children's Project. Responsibilities included preparing posters, promoting walk to students, encouraging them to participate and ensuring their safety on the day.

OTHER INFORMATION

Full Clean Driving Licence.

Qualified First-Aider.

REFERENCES

Mr Ger O'Brien, Manager, Xtravision, Kells, Co Kildare.
Tel: xxxxxx.

Mr John O'Neill, Vice Principal, Kells Community College, Kells, Co Kildare. Tel: xxxxx.

How to structure your CV

> Put your personal details here. Your name is the most important detail so highlight it with a large bold font.

My Name

Personal Details

HINTS

- *If you have an unusual name, e.g. some Irish names, it may be useful to state gender for employers who are not familiar with your name such as employers based abroad.*
- *Date of birth is optional .*
- *You are not required to include gender, nationality or religion, as they should not influence an employer's decision.*

My Personal Skills Statement

It is useful to include a short statement (no more than 2 sentences) that summarises your skills, qualities or career objective. It gives the employer a quick picture of your main selling points and you can use the rest of the CV to support this statement. Two or three short bullet points could also do this. (see sample CVs)

My Education Details

> Transfer the relevant information from your school experience summary into this section.

Schools attended in reverse order, exams undertaken or to be undertaken, actual results and expected results. Tell the employer about projects, essays and other special achievements or interests that you may have in school.

HINTS

- *You may include your expected Leaving Cert. results. Make sure that they are realistic – there is no point saying that you expect an A2 in History if your results to date have been C1.*
- *A table is useful for listing results (see sample CVs).*
- *If you know what you want to do after second level, include a statement such as ' I hope to pursue a business qualification in third level and develop a career in business on completion of that course'.*
- *Your involvement in projects/group work tells an employer about you as an individual. They will ask you questions about these in an interview.*
- *If you have any special interests or achievements as part of your education, tell the employer.*
- *Computer skills are always important. If you have used computers for school projects say it, and the package used, e.g. Microsoft Word, Microsoft Excel, etc.*

My Work Experience

> Transfer the relevant information from your work experience summary into this section.

Put down the most recent first, i.e. reverse chronological order. Include dates, names of employers and your responsibilities listing specific achievements and successes.

HINTS

- *Include voluntary work and work in a family business, farm, relation's business etc. Sometimes people take this for granted, however, it is very useful work experience and often means greater responsibilities than you would get from an unrelated employer.*
- *Give details of your duties, responsibilities, and results achieved.*
- *Areas of responsibilities that employers are interested in are: responsibility for keys, cash, or other staff (including training other staff)? This shows that an employer trusted you with their premises, their money or other staff.*
- *Do not use 'I'. Say 'Responsible for' instead of 'I was responsible for'.*

My Extra-curricular and Other Activities

Details listing specific responsibilities and successes

Transfer the relevant information from your extra-curricular/other experience summary into this section.

HINTS

- *Say your level of involvement with the club and posts of responsibilities that you may have held. If you have achieved results, include these, e.g. you may have attained grades in music or sport.*
- *You may have been involved where a group of people organised an activity such as a trip, a play, an open-day, a workshop etc. – state your involvement and what the result was. This may just be a result where people went on a trip and enjoyed themselves.*

Other Information/Achievements

This is a useful catch all where you can include your computing skills, language skills, driving licence etc.

HINTS

- *Include usage of computer packages, Internet etc. – state if you have achieved grades or certificates.*
- *Include your ability to speak a foreign language(s) – state your level of competence i.e. 'Junior Cert. French' or 'conversational French' as a result of spending a 3-week holiday there.*
- *Activities that do not fall into the previous three headings, can be included here.*

References

A list of people (generally two names – one school and one employment) who are willing to recommend you to an employer.

HINT

- *Contact these people to ask for their permission first.*

Put a date and signature on your CV. This lets the employer see how neat your handwriting is and will also allow you to remember when you did the CV.

Step 2.

Start typing now!

Use the suggested layout to start typing your CV now. The information you included in your experience summary worksheets should give you loads of information to include in your CV.

Tips

Typing – Type first and edit later, many people change their work as they type. The end result is that you end up with a small amount of text after an hour's work. It is better to type two or three pages first and then go back over what you have written and edit it in one go.

Step 3. **Edit and edit again**

Now that you have written the first draft, it is time to edit your CV. This is the point where you take out information that you feel is not relevant, change around the layout of your CV, rewrite sentences that don't make sense etc.

Tips

Because you are so familiar with your CV at this point, it is useful to get a friend, parent or teacher to look at your CV and fill out the checklist as well. This gives you somebody else's opinion which is really what the employer who gets your CV will be doing.

Worksheet | **CV Editing**

- *Complete this CV editing worksheet to make sure that you have followed the basic rules of completing a CV.*
- *Look at the sample CVs on pages 50, 51, 52 and 53 and compare them to your CV.*
- *Look at the positive words and expressions on page 59 to make sure that you have included words that apply to you.*

CV rules – Style	Yes/No	Suggestions for improvement
My CV looks good at first glance.		
My CV looks professional.		
Dates and events are in reverse order.		
My CV is no more than two A4 pages.		
I use headlines.		
I use bullet points.		
My CV does not look cluttered, and there are no large blank spaces.		

CV rules – Substance	Yes/No	Suggestions for improvement
I have included positive items only.		
So what? If I was an employer, would I be impressed by the information in the CV?		
My skills and achievements are clearly described and supported by facts.		
All the information is relevant and accurate.		
Very few sentences are starting with 'I'. e.g. I was responsible for… etc.		
The information is true and accurate.		
There is adequate contact information, i.e. address and phone numbers.		
I have used correct grammar, spelling and punctuation.		

IMPORTANT NOTE: *for Leaving Certificate Vocational Programme (LCVP) and Leaving Certificate Applied students (LCA).* Check with your teacher to make sure that the CV you have now produced meets the assessment guidelines laid down by the Department of Education for the assessment of your CV as part of your portfolio submission in the final examination of your subject.

Step 4. Revise and update your CV – the never-ending CV

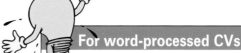

The CV that you have produced now is the starting copy of a CV that you will change continually over the next 10, 20, even 30 years depending on how many times you change careers or apply for jobs in that time. As you increase your education, work and other experiences, you will add more information to your CV and delete out-of-date information. In your CV, your most recent achievements are the most important, for example if you get a third level qualification in the future, you will probably delete your Junior Cert. results from your CV to make room for your third-level results.

For word-processed CVs

1. Use common package such as Microsoft Word.

2. Use spell check and grammar check.

3. For the 'body' text use business fonts such as Times New Roman, Verdana, Arial, Tahoma. Use a 10, 11 or 12 font size.

4. Use underline, Larger Text or CAPITAL LETTERS for headings.

5. Use bold or italics to emphasise achievements in the main body of the CV, etc.

6. Tables are useful for exam results etc. If you are using a table, make sure that most lines are not visible.

7. Print on good quality paper.

8. Print should be **BLACK**. Other colours are not acceptable.

How Employers Short-list CVs

Yes Interview   Maybe Interview   No Interview

When an employer has to process a large number of CVs. They first read each CV quickly and make an initial decision. They will decide that the CV should go into one of three piles:

- CVs that are definite 'yes interview'.
- Those that are 'maybe interview'.
- CVs that are definite 'no interview'.

The employer will often go through the first two piles of CVs again to:

- confirm their decision for the definite 'yes interview',
- make a final judgement on the 'maybe interview'.

The decision to upgrade a 'maybe CV' will depend on how many are in the 'yes' pile or if they see something in the CV which they missed in their initial reading. Employers do not usually look at the 'no interview' pile a second time. Some large employers may get a second person to review the 'no' pile just to make sure that they have not missed anything.

Your CV's job is to be in the 'YES INTERVIEW' pile.

Yes Interview

POSITIVE WORDS TO USE FOR JOB SEEKING

Positive ways to describe yourself

When writing your CV or application form, try to avoid starting sentences with 'I', for example, 'I am good at . . . '
'I was responsible for. . . '. It gets very repetitive especially when using bullet points. Start with a verb, noun or
adjective, for example:

- Skillful communicator
- High degree of ability in electrical tasks
- Very good at doing a variety of tasks efficiently
- Exceptional at motivating large or small groups
- Have a talent for numerical work
- Familiar with a wide range of computer software
- Qualified to teach gymnastics up to level 3

Useful other ways to describe yourself include:

Adept at . . .	An expert in . . .	Competent in . . .	Exceptional at . . .
Skilled at . . .	with the ability to . . .	Very good at . . .	A talent for . . .
Excelling at . . .	Possessing a high	An experienced . . .	Familiar with . . .
A skilful . . .	degree of ability in . . .	Extremely good at . . .	Qualified to . . .

Positive action words

Finding the right words can be one of the hardest parts of writing to an employer. The following list includes positive
action words that are useful for your CV. These are words that you can use to describe actions, responsibilities and
achievements. Look back at your CV and summary sheets to make sure you have used some of them.

Accessed	Compiled	Eliminated	Hired	Mentored	Promoted	Scheduled
Achieved	Completed	Enabled	Identified	Monitored	Proposed	Secured
Acquired	Conducted	Established	Implemented	Motivated	Provided	Selected
Acted	Consulted	Evaluated	Improved	Negotiated	Purchased	Set Up
Administered	Contributed	Executed	Increased	Opened	Recommended	Shaped
Advised	Controlled	Exercised	Initiated	Operated	Recorded	Sold
Analysed	Co-ordinated	Expanded	Installed	Organised	Recruited	Solved
Appointed	Correlated	Expedited	Instructed	Oversaw	Reduced	Structured
Arranged	Created	Explored	Interacted	Participated	Reorganised	Supervised
Assigned	Delegated	Facilitated	Invented	Performed	Reported	Taught
Attended	Demonstrated	Formulated	Investigated	Pioneered	Represented	Tested
Booked	Designed	Founded	Launched	Planned	Researched	Trained
Budgeted	Determined	Generated	Led	Prepared	Resolved	Upgraded
Checked	Developed	Guided	Liaised	Presented	Restored	Used
Coached	Devised	Handled	Maintained	Processed	Restructured	Utilised
Communicated	Edited	Headed	Managed	Produced	Revised	Won
Competed	Effected	Helped	Marketed	Programmed	Saved	Wrote

NOTE: **Most of the words above are in the past tense (they end in 'ed') because they describe things that
you have done in the past. Change the 'ed' to 'ing' if you want to use them in the present tense.**

Positive qualities

The following words describe characteristics that employers look for in their staff. Even though many are obvious, they are words that can easily be left out of your CV/application form. Use them in your summary worksheets, when writing your CV, application form or covering letter and include them in your interview practice sessions.

While it is important to use the words, you must also be able to give the employer proof, i.e. examples, of using these qualities.

Able	Diplomatic	Knowledgeable	Punctual	Supportive
Accurate	Dynamic	Loyal	Qualified	Tactful
Adaptable	Effective	Mature	Quick	Talented
Adventurous	Efficient	Methodical	Quick-thinking	Tenacious
Alert	Energetic	Motivated	Rational	Thorough
Ambitious	Enthusiastic	Objective	Realistic	Thoughtful
Analytical	Fast	Open-minded	Reliable	Trustworthy
Articulate	Firm	Organised	Resourceful	Versatile
Assertive	Flexible	Outgoing	Responsible	Well-groomed
Bright	Friendly	Patient	Self-assured	Willing
Calm	Gregarious	People-orientated	Self-confident	Witty
Capable	Hardworking	Perceptive	Self-motivated	
Competent	Honest	Persistent	Self-reliant	
Confident	Humane	Personable	Sensitive	
Consistent	Imaginative	Pioneering	Skilled	
Creative	Independent	Practical	Smart	
Decisive	Informed	Principled	Spirited	
Dedicated	Innovative	Productive	Stable	
Dependable	Intelligent	Professional	Strong	
Diligent	Inventive	Proficient	Successful	

Positive qualities that employers look for

Employers like people who are:

Able to follow instructions accurately	Accurate	Organised	Tidy in their appearance
	Enthusiastic	Positive	Trustworthy
Able to handle problems	Friendly	Proud of their work	Use their initiative
Able to work as part of a team	Flexible	Punctual	Willing to learn
Able to work with customers	Motivated	Reliable	

Employers don't want to employ people who are:

Arrogant	Dour and unfriendly	Lacking enthusiasm	Unreliable
Bad timekeepers	Disorganised	Lacking motivation	Not willing to follow instructions
Constant complainers	Irresponsible	Sloppy in appearance	

COMPLETING AN APPLICATION FORM

The function of an application form

An application form has the same job as a CV – to get you an interview. The employer uses the application form to get information from candidates and will short-list on the basis of that information.

The difference between an application form and a CV

The big difference between an application form and a CV is that the employer has some control over the information that you put on an application form. For example, employers can insist that you put detailed exam results on their application form, whereas you can be selective about this when completing your CV. Application forms make the applicant concentrate on the areas that the employer is interested in.

Why employers use application forms

Larger employers who get a high number of candidates often use application forms. They allow the employer to structure the applicant's information in an organised manner that make it easier to compare applicants and draw up a short list for interview.

How employers design application forms

Generally, application forms are divided into two sections.

SECTION ONE – tell me your facts
This is for facts such as:

- **Personal details** – date of birth, address, phone number, contact information etc.
- **Education details** – subjects studied, grades received etc.
- **Work experience details** – dates worked, main duties, name of employer etc.

This is a straightforward part of the form as the information needed is facts such as dates, names, grades etc.

 NOTE: Some application forms, especially those for part-time or temporary employment will only ask for this information.

SECTION TWO – tell me why you should get the job

In this part of the form, the employer wants to find out about your qualities, skills and experience relevant to the job? They want to find out what you can do for them as a potential employee. They try to get a picture of you in relation to your skills in the workplace, your personal qualities and your interest in the job.

They will be very interested in special interests and achievements that you may have, but which the other questions in the application form did not give you an opportunity to promote. Generally, the questions allow you to provide as much information as you feel is relevant with the only limitation being the amount of blank space available for your answer.

This is the most important part of the form because the answers you give will directly affect the employers decision whether or not to interview you (assuming that you meet the minimum requirements and your application is professionally presented). It is also the most difficult part of the form to fill out and needs plenty of practice.

3-Step Process to Completing an Application Form

Step 1. **Prepare** – Find out about the job and list the experiences, skills and qualities that you have to offer it.

Step 2. **Practise** completing the form. Write practice answers for the questions on it.

Step 3. **Complete the actual form** that you are going to send to the employer.

Step 1. Prepare

You have done a lot of the preparation already!

1. Use the understanding job advertisement worksheet on page 10 to find out about the job and the important skills and qualities that the employer is looking for.

2. Look over your experience summary worksheets to identify your experiences, skills and qualities that will be of benefit to the job. List out the ones that you think are especially relevant to this job on a sheet of paper.

Step 2. Practice

Before you complete the final form you should complete some practice forms. Some tips on completing practice application forms are:

- Make photocopies of the form so that you have something to practise on.

- Read the instructions carefully and make sure that you understand them fully.

- Answer the straightforward questions first. These are questions that require facts, e.g. name, address, telephone number, education etc.

- Use the information in your summary worksheets to help you answer questions about employment, school projects, your skills etc.

- For questions that need a descriptive or essay-type answer, write a few practice answers on a blank sheet first.

The Worksheets in the following pages will help you practise completing application forms.

Completing an Application Form
THE GOLDEN RULES

 RULE 1

A great application form must have:
- **SUBSTANCE** – It has clear facts about you and your potential.
- **STYLE** – It looks professional, is easy to read and highlights your key skills instantly.

 RULE 2

Always fill out a few practice forms before you fill out the real application.

RULE 3

Read and follow the instructions carefully – only do what you are asked to do. If there are two or three parts to a question make sure to answer each part.

 RULE 4

Your application must be presented in a manner that is easy to read and highlights your key skills instantly. Simple things to make your application look better are:

- Writing should be clear and legible.
- Write clearly and use a strong black pen.
- Spelling should be correct.
- Use bullet points instead of paragraphs – they are easier to read.
- Make sure the form is neat – no finger smudges, coffee stains etc.

Application form practice worksheets

Worksheet 1 'Tell me your facts' sheet

This will help you to practise filling out the 'tell me your facts' part of an application form . When you have to fill out a real application form, just transfer the information from this worksheet to the relevant sections of the application form.

Please complete all the sections below. Write legibly using a black pen.

APPLICANT DETAILS

Name _____

Address _____

_____

_____

_____

Telephone _____

Mobile (*if applicable*) _____

Email (*if applicable*) _____

Date of Birth (*optional*) _____

EDUCATIONAL DETAILS

School names and addresses

_____

_____

_____

Dates attended

_____

_____

_____

JUNIOR CERTIFICATE RESULTS   Year exam taken:

Subject	level	Grade

LEAVING CERTIFICATE RESULTS   Year exam taken (*due to be taken if applicable*):

Subject	level	Grade Achieved (or expected grade if applicable)

Get Your Ideal Job

Worksheet 1 continued from overleaf

WORK HISTORY (include all work including voluntary work)

Name and Address of Employer	Type of business	Brief description of responsibilities and achievements	Dates From	To

INTERESTS AND EXTRA-CURRICULAR ACTIVITIES

Describe activity	Club membership (*if applicable*)	Your level of involvement

KEYBOARD / COMPUTING SKILLS

Packages used	Level of proficiency (*basic, good or advanced*)

DRIVING LICENCE (tick relevant box)

Full Licence ❑   Provisional *(for how long)* ❑ _____   No driving licence ❑

REFERENCES (names of people who are familiar with your work, personal or academic abilities who the employer can ask for a reference)

Name _____   Occupation_____

Address_____   Telephone number_____

_____

Name _____   Occupation_____

Address_____   Telephone number_____

_____

Worksheet 2 'Tell me why you should get the job' sheet.

The following questions are common questions used by employers in application forms. Do this exercise for each question.

1. Read the question carefully.

2. Look at your summary sheets to get ideas on what to include in the answer. Think about your experiences, skills and achievements that are relevant to that job. Bear in mind the skills and qualities that the employer may be looking for.

3. On a blank sheet of paper write out a possible answer. If necessary rewrite your answer until you feel that you have the best answer. Remember to use bullet points if possible and keep your answer short – it must fit into the space provided on the form!

4. Hand-write your final answer onto the worksheet. Use a black pen and write clearly.

The questions can apply to any job. Your answer should be for a job or career that you are interested in, or intend to apply for, in the future.

Name the job or career that you have chosen for the purpose of answering these questions:

Why do you think that you are a suitable candidate for this job?

Pick three skills you have that are relevant to this job. Give one example of how you have applied each skill to a work, school or other/extra-curricular activity.

What has your best personal achievement been to date and why?

Give a brief description of the activities you do outside of school or work. Why do you like these activities?

Step 3. **Fill out the actual form and send it**

At this point, you will have done your preparation, filled out some practice forms and have answers that you are happy with for the general questions on the form.

You are now ready to complete the final version of your application and send it to the employer. Take care to complete it neatly and not to make any mistakes.

Some suggestions after you have finished the form:

- Get somebody to read your form before you send it off – they might spot errors that you missed.
- Keep a copy of the completed form for future use and in preparation for an interview.
- Get a receipt from the post office if you are posting the form to the employer.

Send the application off and the best of luck with it. Hopefully it will get you an interview or at least to the next part of the recruitment process.

Online applications

Online applications are becoming very popular with larger employers. This is especially so for the recruitment of third-level students and in industries that are computer-friendly, e.g. computing, electronics, banking, consultancy etc. Online recruitment agencies also use online applications and CVs extensively.

Basically an online application is an electronic version of a paper application. The questions are similar and you use the same steps that we have used for paper application forms.

Electronic short-listing

Sometimes employers use a computer package to scan applications for key words. Read the information about the job carefully and try to include as many of the important words used in the job information on your application as possible.

Keywords can be specified results, computer packages or languages. They may also be certain skills or qualities such as teamwork, leadership, communication etc. Remember, however, that an application with loads of keywords but very few examples of using them, will not get far.

Some tips for applying for a job by online application

- Print out a copy of the online application form and complete it by hand before doing the real thing.
- Complete the form in exactly the same way as you would a paper application form.
- Use your summary worksheets to identify the information to include in the application form.
- Short sentences and bullet points are easier to read than long paragraphs. This is especially true when reading from a computer screen.
- Before submitting the completed application, print out the final version and check your spelling and grammar. It may also be useful to get somebody to look at it for you before you hit the Send button.

Tips for applying by email and making your CV more scannable are listed on page 71.

WRITING A COVERING LETTER

The function of a Covering Letter

A covering letter is often the first point of contact between you and an employer. The covering letter is a summary of the reasons why the employer should seriously consider you for the job. Your CV or application form will give the employer detailed information about you.

The job of a covering letter is to give the employer a very positive impression of you and to encourage them to:

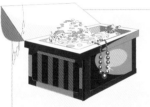

- read the letter,
- look at your CV or application form,
- call you for interview.

When to use covering letters

While you can send the same CV to a large number of different employers, a covering letter should be written to apply directly to the company and the job for which you are applying. The covering letter is a great way of personalising your job application to an individual job.

You should use a covering letter in practically all situations when you are applying for a job. This is the case whether you are applying by application form, by CV, replying to a job advertisement or sending a speculative application. If you are sending your CV electronically you should use a covering email which is effectively an electronic version of a covering letter.

Writing a Covering Letter
THE GOLDEN RULES

 RULE 1

A great covering letter must have:
- **SUBSTANCE** – It has clear facts about you and your potential.
- **STYLE** – It looks professional, is easy to read and highlights your key skills instantly.

 RULE 2

Your covering letter is effectively a summary of your application. It should give a clear overview of the skills and experiences you have that are relevant to the job you are applying for.

 RULE 3

Your letter should be no more than one page in length, with a maximum of 4 to 5 paragraphs.

 RULE 4

A covering letter is a business document and should be typed or word processed, unless you are specifically asked for a handwritten letter. If you are asked for a handwritten letter, make sure your writing is neat and legible.

 RULE 5

Address your letter to a named person. Try to find out the name of the person who is looking after the job. Ring the company reception if necessary. If you cannot find out the name of the person who will be dealing with your application, start with 'Dear Sir / Madam'.

 RULE 6

Always use good quality, A4 paper. If possible use paper that is more than 100 grams in weight or bond paper. Sometimes, people use coloured paper, however, a high quality white paper always looks professional.

3-Step Process to Completing a Covering Letter

Step 1. **Prepare** – find out about the job and list the main experiences, skills and qualities that you have to offer it.

Step 2. **Write/type a draft letter** so that you have a basic text to work on.

Step 3. **Edit your final version** of the letter and post it.

Step 1. Prepare

1. Do not start writing your letter until after you have completed your CV or application form. The letter is a summary of your CV/application. Read through your CV/application form and highlight the main points that you should include in the covering letter on a sheet of paper.

2. Find out about the job and what the employer wants. Use the job advertisement analysis worksheet on page 10 to find out about the job and the important skills and qualities that you should mention in the covering letter.

Step 2. Write/type a draft letter

Use the suggested layout on the next page to start typing/writing your letter.

Remember, you will get your letter finished quicker if you have something to edit. The greatest time-waster when writing anything is looking at a blank screen or sheet of paper and wondering what to write. The information you need to include is on your CV / application form, so start writing now – you can improve it over time.

Look at the following sample letter to get a general idea of the layout and text of a covering letter. More sample letters are on page 70.

Mr Séan O'Brien
Personnel Manager
Trabolgan Holiday Centre
Midleton
Co Cork

24 April 2007

Dear Mr O'Brien,

I am currently a fifth-year student at the CBS in Midleton and am keen to secure a job for the summer. Having looked at your website, I believe that I possess all the qualities outlined in your profile for a Leisure Assistant.

I have experience of working on teams through my involvement with the local GAA club. I am a member of the U18 hurling team and also assist in training the children on the U12 panel. Having worked as a waiter in Midleton Park Hotel last summer, I am proficient at working in a pressurised environment and dealing with the public in a friendly and efficient manner. I am a member of Midleton Leisure Centre and am a strong swimmer. I would be very keen to undertake lifeguard training at Trabolgan on a voluntary basis.

Enclosed please find my Curriculum Vitae. From Monday, 4 June until the end of August, I will be available for full-time work. I hope that you will look favourably on my application and am available for interview at your convenience.

Yours sincerely,

_____

Shane Beecher

How to structure your covering letter

This is a suggested layout for your covering letter. It is useful to scribble out the main points you want to say in your letter on the right-hand side of this page. The best way to complete a covering letter is to start writing a draft letter which you can then edit and improve as you go. Start typing now and use the structure below as a basis for your letter. The sample letters on pages 68 and 70 will also give you some ideas.

Name, title and address of person to
whom letter is being sent.
If you don't know, find out. Leave out the
address if you are stuck for space.

Your address
Date
Telephone number

Salutation – Dear . . . *Is it Mr, Ms, Miss or Mrs Jones?*

Opening paragraph – (one or two sentences at most). *Tell the employer why you are writing, e.g. name the job that you are applying for and mention how you found out about it.*

Middle paragraph – (Maximum of 5/6 sentences). *Sell yourself to the employer.*

Give a brief summary of your career to date and relevant work experience that you may have. Make sure that the information is positive and highlights skills that are useful to the job. Show the employer how you can be of direct benefit to them. You could also use bullet points to highlight key points in this paragraph.

Your Job analysis and summary worksheets will help you identify items to include in this paragraph. Check the list of action verbs and skills in pages 59 and 60 to get useful words to use in the letter.

Note: *Sometimes it is better to split this into two paragraphs. The first paragraph is to highlight your career and achievements to date and the second paragraph is to highlight your suitability for the job.*

Closing paragraph – (one or two sentences at most). *Close off politely referring to the enclosed CV or application form. It is useful to restate your interest in the job and in working for this employer. This paragraph wraps up the letter and is the place to try to get the employer to commit to some action.*

Closing Salutation: *Yours sincerely, Sincerely, Yours Truly, etc.*

Your Signature
with Name typed underneath it

See sample letters on next page for some ideas.

SAMPLE COVERING LETTERS

Ms Una Roche,
Manager,
Spanish Point Restaurant,
Main Street,
Wexford.

2 May 2007

Dear Ms Roche,

I am a student at the Community College in Wexford and will complete Transition Year in June. I wish to apply for a job as a waitress in your restaurant for the summer.

Recently I undertook two weeks work experience at the Tourist Office in Wexford and learnt how to deal with queries in a friendly and efficient manner. I am proficient at juggling a number of tasks at the same time. In school, I have maintained a strong academic record while competing successfully to All Ireland level in athletics. I am also capable of adapting to new situations and learning quickly.

Enclosed please find my Curriculum Vitae. I would welcome the opportunity to meet with you to discuss my application further. If no opportunities currently exist, I would appreciate if you would retain my Curriculum Vitae on file and consider me for positions that arise in the future.

Yours sincerely,

Eimear Reynolds

Step 3. Edit your final version of the letter

Now send it to the employer. Don't forget to include the CV or application form. Keep a copy of all that you have sent including the letter. Use a good quality envelope and address the envelope properly! Also make sure that you put the correct value stamp on it, you don't want the employer's first impression to be 'this person does not know how to send a letter properly!'

Ms Jane McNamara
Manager
Daly's Mini-Market
Pembroke Street
Ballinasloe
Co Galway

25 April 2007

Dear Ms McNamara,

I wish to apply for the position of Sales Assistant as advertised in 'name of local paper' on Friday, 27 April. I am currently a fifth-year student in St Mary's in Ballinasloe and am available for part-time work. I will be available for full-time work from Monday, 4 June until the end of August.

Given the opportunity, I believe that I could be a very effective employee. Having acted as a cashier for the TSB school bank this year, I have experience of handling money and dealing with customers. I have experience of teamwork through my involvement in the school basketball and hockey teams. I also have strong leadership and interpersonal skills as demonstrated by my election as Class Prefect and my subsequent achievements in that role.

Enclosed is my Curriculum Vitae, which outlines my skills and experience in more detail. I would welcome the opportunity to meet with you to discuss my application further.

Yours sincerely,

Joanne Morrissey

USEFUL TIPS FOR MAKING ELECTRONIC APPLICATIONS

Applying by email

Because the use of email has increased across most business sectors, it is now acceptable to apply for most vacancies by email.

Guidelines for applying for a job by covering email with your CV as an attachment:

- While emails tend to be informal, your application is a business document and the language you use should reflect this. Your email is really just an electronic version of a cover letter. The text of the email should be the same as you would include in a covering letter.
- A letter that looks well on paper can look cluttered and long on a computer screen so you may need to make the email shorter than your letter.
- Sending a CV as an attachment may mean that you lose your formatting. Use a common word processing package and keep the formatting plain. Left align the text and avoid using tabs. Some employers will insist that you send a text-only version.
- Bullet points are easier to read onscreen than long paragraphs.
- The receiver of your email may see a completely different layout to your email than the layout you send. Be aware of this when writing a covering email – use plain font and keep the formatting simple.
- Use spell check and remember to attach the document before you send the email.

Making your CV scannable

Some employers use computer-scanning software to short-list applications. They scan the CV attachments for keywords, e.g. types of skills, names of computer applications etc. Make doubly sure that you include these key words in any electronic application you make. If you want to make your CV more scannable, the following points may help:

- If you know or suspect that a company may be scanning CVs, post two versions, using a Post-It note to indicate the scannable version.
- Use keywords in the CV. Analyse the job advertisement to identify the keywords relevant to the job see pages 8 and 10.
- A scannable paper CV is basically stripped of all formatting.
  - Use a basic sans-serif font (such as Helvetica/ Arial).
  - No italics, script, underlining, bullets.
  - No graphics, shading, multiple columns, vertical lines.
- Use a high-quality printer and plain white paper.
- Put heading information on separate lines.

Tips for making online applications are listed on page 66.

PART 4

TALKING TO EMPLOYERS

CONTENTS

(i) Completing a job interview

- The structure of a job interview
- Interviews – the employer's perspective
- Four-step process to a completing a job interview
- Preparing for a job interview – worksheet
- Practice interview worksheets
- Dealing with interview nerves

(ii) How interviewers interview

(iii) Job interviews by telephone

- Four-step process to completing a job interview by telephone

(iv) Using the telephone for job seeking

It's good to talk!

All the activities that you have done so far have been geared to applying for a job by paper or electronically – letter, email, CV, application form etc. If you made a mistake or wanted to improve it – you simply changed it on the page. The next part of this book concentrates on a different aspect of job seeking – talking to an employer.

What's the difference between writing to and talking to an employer?

You don't get a second chance when you are talking to an employer. You must make a positive impression from the start and be able to talk openly about your skills.

The information that you put into your summary worksheets is what you will talk to the employer about, but:

- Speaking about your skills is a different challenge to writing them down on a sheet of paper.
- While a CV can be applied to many vacancies, an interview relates to an individual job or employer.

In this section, we discuss some simple and effective ways for you to prepare for a conversation with an employer. This could be a formal interview, a telephone conversation or a casual meeting. The worksheets and exercises will help you to practise:

- speaking about your skills and experiences,
- proving that you have those skills by mentioning relevant examples,
- relating your skills to the job in question.

They will help you talk to an employer in a way that will convince them that you are the best person for the job!

COMPLETING A JOB INTERVIEW

The purpose of a job interview

An interview is basically a communication between two people – you and the employer. In its simplest form, it could be described as a one-sided conversation with the employer asking the questions. The purpose is to find out information about you (the job seeker). The employer then makes a decision on the basis of that information – will they give you a job or not?

REMEMBER You will only be asked to go to an interview if the employer thinks that you can do the job in the first place. During the interview, you must convince the employer that you can do that job better than anyone else.

The structure of a job interview

A job interview can be broken down into 4 parts.

The Start – This is the 'settling in' part where the interviewer asks you some straightforward questions to make you comfortable. First impressions are vital.

The Middle – We now get down to business. The interviewer asks you detailed questions about your skills, experiences and what you have to offer the job. They want to get a better knowledge of you. While the interviewer may be asking lots of questions, there is one question on their mind – **'Should you get the job?'**

The End – An interviewer will thank you for coming and give you an opportunity to ask them questions. They will tell you what the next stage of the process is, when they will contact you about the result of the interview, etc.

The Decision – The final decision is made after all the interviews, but interviewers use the time immediately after each interview to make notes about that candidate to help them make the final decision.

Many interviewers will rate each candidate under headings such as the key skills for the job, other requirements, etc. (see page 8 – What do employers want?). At the end of the day, the interviewer(s) then compare(s) each candidate under those headings and a final decision is made about who gets the job.

Interviews – the employer's perspective

At an interview, the employer has one simple question –

'Why should I give this job to you?'

Every question that the employer asks is to answer this one question. The candidate who answers it best is the one who gets the job. This question can be broken down into three parts.

1. **Can you do the job?**
   Do you have the skills and ability for the job, what parts of the job can you do immediately and what parts will you need to learn?

2. **Will you do the job?**
   How interested and motivated are you are in the job?

3. **Will you fit in?**
   Employers place a lot of emphasis on making sure that new employees fit smoothly into the workplace and get on with other staff (including the boss!) and customers.

'Why should I give this job to you?'

You must convince the employer that you are the best person for the job. That means telling the employer that:

- **You can do the job best** – you have the skills and experience to do the job and have examples to prove it.
- **You want the job most** – you are motivated to do this job.
- **You will 'fit in'** – because of your positive attitude and interpersonal skills.

4-Step Process to Completing a Job Interview

Step 1. **Prepare** – Convert your written preparation into 'Talk Language'.

Step 2. **Practise** speaking about yourself and your skills.

Step 3. **Get the basics right** – dress, posture, eye contact etc.

Step 4. **Do the interview** – look the part, speak clearly, project confidence and enthusiasm for the job.

Step 1. Prepare

You have already done some preparation – by completing your experience summary worksheets, you identified skills and experiences that you have to offer the employer. You also have examples to prove that you used those skills.

However, in an interview situation, you want to:

- talk confidently about your skills and experiences,
- give the interviewer evidence (examples) of using those skills, and
- describe how your skills and experiences relate to the job.

You want to do this in a way that will convince the employer that you are the best person for the job – BUT you have only a short time – most interviews are less than 20 minutes long. This is a short time in which to say all the things you want to tell the employer – Preparation is vital!

What you have to do is convert the information that you have about yourself and the job into **'talk language'** so that you are comfortable talking about yourself to other people. The worksheets in the following pages will help you to do this.

Why do I need to convert it into 'talk language'?

Think about a recent conversation that you have had with a friend about sport, school, music etc. Look at the statements below and tick the ones that apply to that conversation:

- ❏ We used single sentences and short paragraphs.
- ❏ Some sentences were not completed because you were interrupted in mid-conversation by the other person.
- ❏ Questions were asked to clarify comments made or words used.
- ❏ The subject of the conversation changed a few times, even if it was a short conversation.

If you wrote out the conversation word for word, would it make sense to the reader? – *No, it probably wouldn't.*

The same is true if you are trying to convert a CV or application form into a conversation, because speaking about yourself and your skills to a potential employer is a very different thing to writing them down on a sheet of paper!

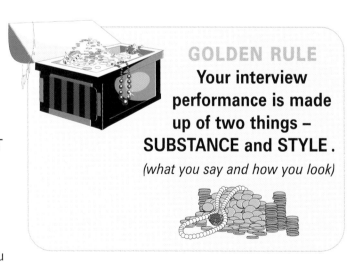

GOLDEN RULE
Your interview performance is made up of two things – SUBSTANCE and STYLE .
(what you say and how you look)

Worksheet | Preparing for a Job Interview

Employers have one basic question 'Why should I give this job to you?' These worksheets will help you pick out the main reasons why the interviewer should give the job to you rather than anybody else.

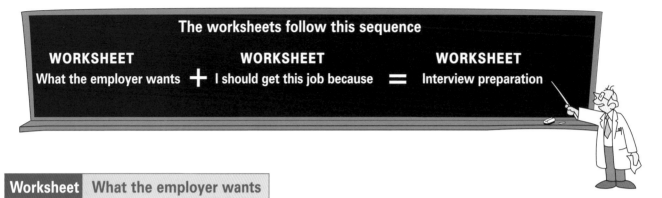

The worksheets follow this sequence

WORKSHEET
What the employer wants **+** **WORKSHEET**
I should get this job because **=** **WORKSHEET**
Interview preparation

Worksheet | What the employer wants

Pick A Job. In order to complete the worksheets, you need to have a specific job in mind. Choose a job that you are interested in, pick a job from the recruitment page of a newspaper or use one of the jobs that you analysed in 'understanding job advertisements' in Part 1.

Name of the job that I am preparing to be interviewed for:

Write out a brief description of the skills, qualities and experiences required for the job

The ideal candidate will have . . .

List the main things that the employer is looking for in a successful candidate for this job? These could be skills, experience or general qualities. Have no more than six bullet points.

Now, look over the list and number each point from 1 to 6 in order of importance.
(1 being the most important and 6 being the least important.) Write your rating in the narrow column on the right.

Worksheet | I should get this job because

Before you start writing! *Read the tasks on the worksheet first. Then look back over your completed summary sheets and make out a rough list of what you want to include in this worksheet.*

Name of the job that I am preparing to be interviewed for:_____

I should get this job because . . . Write out up to six main reasons why you should get this job? These can be your skills, experience or general qualities. Bear in mind what you included in the previous worksheet 'What the employer wants'.		

Now, look over the above reasons why you should get the job and number each point from 1 to 6 in order of importance.
(1 being the most important and 6 being the least important.) Write your rating in the narrow column on the right.

By completing those two worksheets, you now have a good idea about:

- what the employer wants,
- what you have to offer this job.

The next thing to do is prepare to talk about what you have to offer the job at an interview. This leads us to the interview preparation worksheets.

The other people being interviewed for the job will also have a list of reasons why they should get the job. Many of their reasons will be the same as yours. (If you want proof, just look at the answers that your friends have given to the worksheet above.)

Interview preparation worksheet

In the job interview, you must convince the interviewer that you are the best person for the job. You do this by:

- telling the interviewer about your skills and experiences,
- proving that you have those skills by giving examples of using those skills and stating the results achieved after using them,
- relating your skills to the job that you are being interviewed for.

The interview preparation worksheet will help you prepare what you want to say in the interview. An interview is a tense situation, you must think on your feet and answer a variety of questions. By using this worksheet to prepare, you will be better able to talk about yourself in an interview.

HOW TO COMPLETE THE INTERVIEW PREPARATION WORKSHEET

The interview preparation worksheet has three columns with the following headings:

COLUMN 1	COLUMN 2	COLUMN 3
One reason why I should get this job *Transfer ONE reason from the worksheet on page 77 into this column. Examples include:* *I should get this job because . . .* ● I have selling skills. ● I am a team player. ● I have experience in dealing with difficult situations. ● I am a good time manager. ● I am willing to work hard.	**Proof that I have this skill** *This separates you from the other candidates who say that they have the same skills as you. Give the employer proof that you have used your skills to get results.* While you only have one reason in column 1, it is useful to have lots of examples in this column. Use your summary worksheets to come up with as many examples as possible. The more examples and results you have, the more you convince the employer that you are good at that activity. Be specific with examples and include results.	**So what? – Relevance to this job** *The fact that you have certain skills and experiences is nice, but what relevance have they to this job? This is the 'So what' factor.* Try to make your experiences and skills relevant to the job you are being interviewed for. Look over your summary worksheets and use them to help you complete this column.

Using examples to prove that you have a skill

● I have selling skills, I sold 200 Christmas cards as part of my responsibilities in the transition year mini company.

● I am a team player, I was a member of the school basketball team that won the regional U16 finals last year.

● I have experience of dealing with difficult situations, I have worked part time at the customer service counter in the local supermarket for the past year.

● I am a good time manager. Last year, I passed my exams, played with the local football club and also worked up to 10 hours per week in a local shop.

● I am willing to work hard, I passed my exams and worked up to 15 hours per week in the family business.

Saying you have a skill and providing evidence of it is much stronger than just saying that I am a good at something – anybody can say they are good at doing things, but not everybody will have the evidence to prove it.

Sample Interview Preparation Worksheet

One reason why I should get this job	Proof/evidence that I have this skill	So what? – Relevance to this job
I have selling skills.	*I sold 200 Christmas cards as part of my responsibilities in the transition year mini company.* *(You will have a number of examples to prove one skill.)*	To a sales job – *I would use my selling skills to meet and perhaps exceed my sales targets.* To an office job – *This shows my ability to get on with other people, which is a basic requirement for any job. It also shows that I will use my initiative to get a result, for example, to make those sales I had to organise a stand in the school canteen.*

Worksheet | **Interview preparation**

There are 4 worksheets, if you need more, write out the headings on a blank sheet of paper.

I should get this job because . . .	Proof that I have this skill	Relevance to this job
Transfer one reason from worksheet 'I should get this job because' into this column (page 77).	Prove that you have this skill or ability by giving examples of how you have used it in the past – give results where possible. You could have 9 or 10 examples of using the skill.	So what? – If you got this job, how would you use this skill or ability in the job?

Worksheet

I should get this job because . . .	Proof that I have this skill	Relevance to this job

Worksheet

I should get this job because …	Proof that I have this skill	Relevance to this job

Tips

Use your experience summary worksheets to help you with columns 2 and 3.

Continued from overleaf

Worksheet

I should get this job because . . .	Proof that I have this skill	Relevance to this job

Worksheet

I should get this job because . . .	Proof that I have this skill	Relevance to this job

Tips

Write an essay – If you find it hard to fill in the boxes, write out a short essay or story about your experience using the headings on the worksheet as the starting point of each paragraph or section of your story.

Step 2. Practise speaking about yourself and your skills

Why practise?

You now have loads of reasons on worksheets and in your head about why you should get the job. But you have not spoken about it much. In the job interview, you have to talk about all the things you have written down so far.

For many people, the first time they talk about 'Why I should get this job' is during the interview. This puts them under pressure because they find that they:

● do not have time to say all the relevant information that you want to say,

● waste time by giving long-winded answers or worse still give short sharp answers which tell the interviewer nothing about 'Why they should get the job',

● talk about general things and do not give the interviewer specific information about themselves,

● lose confidence during the interview because they feel they are not making sense.

If you are used to talking about yourself, then it will be easier to talk in a job interview.

How to practise

The only way to practise for an interview is to speak about yourself **aloud**. There are two options for doing this:

1. Ask yourself interview questions and answer them to yourself aloud! *(Note: it is less embarrassing if you do this in private.)*

2. Get somebody else, a friend, parent or classmate to ask you interview questions and answer them aloud as if you were in a real interview.

The worksheet on the next page will help you practise interviews.

REMEMBER The best candidate may not get the job if they do an average interview, but an average candidate who does the best interview could get the job.

Who controls a job interview?

The interviewer! – How? They ask the questions.

Think about your conversations with others, both people will ask questions during the discussion. Asking questions is an important part of everyday conversation. It allows us to:

● clarify the other persons views,

● question something they say if we don't understand it,

● change the topic if it is running out of steam.

In a job interview, you give up your right to ask questions and allow the interviewer to ask as many questions as they wish. This is a very important point when preparing for an interview and one that you should bear in mind throughout this section.

Exercise

Record an interview on TV or Radio. It can be any type of interview – current affairs, sports, celebrity etc. Answer the following:

1. Write a brief description of the interview situation.

2. What are the main points that the interviewee is trying to make?

3. Is the interviewer allowing them to make those points? Explain your answer.

4. Is the interviewee answering the questions they are asked or are they saying what they want to say without regard to the questions?

5. Who controlled the interview – the interviewer or interviewee? How did they control it?

Worksheet | Practice interview

This worksheet is designed to help you practise interviews: it contains general questions that you may be asked at an interview. Look at each question and answer it aloud to yourself or get a friend to ask them. After each answer, rate your answer on the worksheet.

REMEMBER

In a job interview, the interviewer wants the answer to one question –

'Why should I give this job to you?'

Every question asked is a 'should you get the job' question in disguise.

'Why should I give this job to you?'

Use every question asked as an opportunity to answer this question. Use the interview preparation worksheets and try to speak your answers in this sequence.

REASON ⇨ PROOF ⇨ RELEVANCE TO JOB

Note to Interviewer: Start the interview with an 'Ice Breaker' such as 'How are you today?' etc. Rate the answers only after you have spoken them aloud.

QUESTIONS	How did the answer sound? Good/Bad/OK	How could the answer be improved? e.g. Did you give a reason why you should get the job? Did you give examples of using a skill with specific results? Did you relate the answer to the job in question?
Tell me about your experiences to date?		
What have you learned from each experience?		
Which experience was the least interesting and why?		
Which experience was most interesting and why?		
Describe your ideal job.		
Why do you want to work here?		
What do you know about this organisation/company?		
Give examples of things you have done in the past that show you can work in a team?		
What kind of people do you prefer to work with?		
What qualities do you like most in a boss?		
How would a friend, teacher, work supervisor describe you?		
What have you done so far that has given you the most satisfaction?		

QUESTIONS	How did the answer sound? Good/Bad/OK	How could the answer be improved? e.g. Did you give a reason why you should get the job? Did you give examples of using a skill with specific results? Did you relate the answer to the job in question?
What is your greatest strength?		
What is your weakness?		
What motivates you?		
How do you normally handle criticism?		
Describe a situation when you: – Had to deal with pressure.		
– Had to adapt to a new or difficult situation.		
– Handled a difficult situation with a co-worker / friend / classmate / customer.		
– Made a bad decision.		
– Made a good decision.		
– Persuaded others to follow your suggestions.		
– Solved a problem.		
What are your career goals?		
Why did you choose your present subjects?		
What subjects did you drop and why?		
What do you hope to do when you finish school/college and why?		
Why should I give this job to you rather than the other candidates?		
Any comments or suggestions how the interview could be improved?		

Step 3. Get the basics right

So far, we have concentrated on the substance (what you say) part of an interview. While this is the important part, how you say it is also important. First impressions make a big difference.

How do first impressions influence an interviewer?

Good first impression. You suggest that you are a strong candidate for the job. The interviewer may use the rest of the interview to back up their first impression.

Bad first impression. You suggest that you are a poor candidate for the job, You spend the rest of the interview trying to change the interviewer's mind – this is very difficult especially if other candidates have made positive impressions.

No first impression. The interview can go either way, but you will be at a disadvantage against a candidate who makes a good first impression and is able to back it up during the interview with proof of their experience and skills.

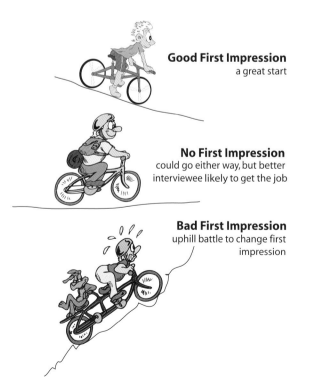

Good First Impression
a great start

No First Impression
could go either way, but better
interviewee likely to get the job

Bad First Impression
uphill battle to change first
impression

How do you make a good first impression at interview?

Dress appropriately. An interview is a business discussion and you should dress to reflect this. Look professional on the day. If you are wearing clothes that you do not normally wear, e.g. a shirt and tie, get used to them by wearing them while you are practising for the interview.

Be well groomed and tidy. Hair tidy, teeth brushed, clothes clean, etc. Be discreet about body jewellery, if you have doubts leave jewellery off for the interview. When you get the job you can wear it as often as you want.

Arrive early. This helps you to relax. While you are waiting you will have a chance to get used to the building and the environment. If the interviews are running early, you might get a longer interview that will benefit you.

Body language is important because it reinforces what you are saying to the interviewer. Simple things to consider are:

- Have a strong firm handshake.

- Look the interviewer in the eye when you are speaking to them. It is very off-putting if a person who is talking to you looks elsewhere at the same time. How much interest are they displaying in the conversation?

- Sit properly – many interviewees try to hide their nervousness by over-emphasising how relaxed they are. They sit in a very relaxed position that gives an impression of complete disinterest in the job. Sit upright and firm, a good way of ensuring this is to sit with the soles of both your feet firmly touching the ground.

- Smile.

'I am really interested in this job.'

Be prepared. If you have not fully prepared or have little knowledge of the job or the company, the employer may assume (quite rightly) that you are not that interested in the job.

Step 4. Do the interview

Well done – you are now ready to do an interview. Make sure to:

- look the part,
- speak clearly,
- project confidence and enthusiasm.

There are a few things that you should be aware of to help you get through the interview.

Dealing with interview nerves

One of the basic feelings that you will feel before and during an interview is nervousness. This is perfectly natural because an interview is a difficult and unusual situation.

The employer expects you to be nervous and will allow for that when they are interviewing you. In many cases, the interviewer won't notice how nervous you are, even though you will be very conscious of it.

Calming nerves

The best way to deal with nerves is to prepare well for the interview. If you have prepared, you will portray confidence and enthusiasm. This will help overcome initial nervousness. As the interview progresses, your confidence will increase because you are giving well-thought-out and practised answers to the interviewer.

Practice for the interview in the same way that you would train for a sports fixture, rehearse for a play, study for an exam etc. The principle is the same – fail to prepare, prepare to fail!

Physical nerves

Sometimes, the signs of your nervousness are physical, for example:

- dry mouth,
- sweating,
- nervous fidgeting with clothes or hair,
- feeling nauseous,
- short of breath.

This happens because your brain is telling your body to prepare for danger ahead. The danger your brain is referring to is the interview, but your body is preparing for physical danger, e.g. a fall. You can overcome this by telling your body that the danger is not physical. Breathing is an effective way to do this. Breathe deeply and slowly, pulling the air into your lungs. This has a calming affect on your body and will help you cope with the nervousness.

Once the interview has started, these physical signs will quickly disappear, especially if you have prepared and practised for the interview.

HOW INTERVIEWERS INTERVIEW

It is useful to look at how the interviewer approaches the interview.

Types of questions

There are two main types of questions:

- Open questions designed to encourage you to talk as much or as little as you wish about the subject matter of the question.

- Closed questions that require a specific answer, e.g. did you have lunch? The answer can only be yes I did or no I didn't. Can you start next Monday? Yes or no. Many questions in exam papers are closed questions – they require a specific answer!

The questions interviewers ask

Most interview questions are open questions because the interviewer wants you to speak about yourself as much as possible. The more information they have about you, the better a decision they can make.

Open questions generally start with ' who, what, where, when, how and why'. You use open questions all the time in your general conversations:

- What did you do last night?
- How did you answer that question?
- Where are you going after school?

You may still get a short answer, but the nature of the question increases your chances of getting a longer response.

Good interviewers use open questions all the time and will ask more open questions about your answers (this is called probing your answers). If they want to clarify something, they will ask a 'closed' question.

Questioning principles used by interviewers

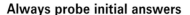

Actions speak louder than words

By asking you about actions and decisions that you took, the interviewer is trying to understand your 'real reason for doing something'. They may ask about choices that you made in school and elsewhere and what other options were available to you at the time.

Always probe initial answers

Interviewers do not take your first answers at face value. They will probe your answer by asking follow-on questions. If you are interested in reading, a good interviewer will ask what books you like to read, how often do you read, what authors do you like to read, why do you like those authors etc. If you really are interested in reading you will be able to answer these questions easily.

Hypothetical questions

Hypothetical questions are when the interviewer tells you about an imaginary situation and asks you how you would deal with that situation. They do this to see how you might react to awkward situations.

Difficult questions

A common difficult interview question is 'What are your weaknesses?' The interviewer wants to see your awareness of your skills and your limitations. A good way to answer this question is to identify a minor weakness and say what actions you have taken to overcome this weakness. For example, 'My essay writing skills are not great, however, I have spoken to the English teacher about this and it is something that I am working to improve this year.'

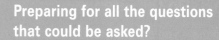

Preparing for all the questions that could be asked?

It is impossible to anticipate all the questions that an interviewer could ask you. The best thing to do is to prepare to answer the fundamental question – Why should you get the job? Every single question that the interviewer asks you is geared towards this. Even a question about your trip to the interview can lead to a reason why you should get the job.

Q. *'How was your bus journey?'*

A. *'It was very nice – It gave me time to think about how I have been interested in this industry since I did my transition work experience in XYZ Company and I am delighted to be given this opportunity here today.'*

That's what is called turning a bus question into an interview question.

The end of the interview

It is important to finish with a good impression. At the end, the interviewer usually asks if you have any questions for them. If you have genuine questions, ask them. If you don't – don't. This is also a good opportunity to sell yourself. If you do not have any questions, it maybe useful to say something like:

'No, I have no questions, I researched the job/company before the interview and I think I have all the information I need. I would like to re-emphasise my genuine interest in the job. I think that I have the skills to do this job well and the ability to learn any other skills required. Thanks for giving me the opportunity to talk to you.'

This is a nice way to leave a good impression with the interviewer. It reinforces everything you have said during the interview.

JOB INTERVIEWS BY TELEPHONE

Why employers use telephone interviews.

Telephone interviews are used by employers for convenience. The phone interview is usually a preliminary interview to short-list candidates for a face-to-face interview later. It is unusual to get a job on the basis of a telephone interview only.

Difference between a telephone job interview and a face-to-face job interview

The big difference is that the employer cannot see you. While you might see this as an advantage because you don't have to dress up, it can create some other challenges:

- What you say is even more important because the employer does not have the benefit of seeing your body language.

- The tone of your voice is important. Think of telephone conversations you have where the other person's tone gives you a negative impression.

- Because the employer is concentrating on your words, you must talk clearly and slowly.

4-Step Process to Completing a Job Interview by Telephone

Step 1. **Prepare** – Find out about the job and list the experiences, skills and qualities that you have to offer it.

Step 2. **Practise** speaking aloud about yourself and your skills.

Step 3. **Get the basics right**

Step 4. **Do the interview** – Sound the part, speak clearly, project confidence and enthusiasm for the job.

Steps 1 and 2. **Prepare and practice**

You prepare for a telephone job interview in the same way as you prepare for a face-to-face interview. Complete the interview preparation worksheets on pages 79 to 80. The principle of what you say in both types of interview is the same – you just use a different method of communication!

Practise using the interview practice worksheet on page 82. If possible, do the practice interviews over the phone as well as face to face.

Step 3. **Get the basics right**

Because the employer cannot see you, grooming and presentation is less important. There are some things you need to look after to make sure the interview goes smoothly.

Quiet room: Make sure that the place where you take the call is quiet with no distractions. Tell other people in the house to stay away from the room for the duration of the call.

Interview preparation worksheets in front of you: The great thing about a telephone interview is that you can bring your notes into the interview. Don't bring too many as it will confuse you, just bring in the interview preparation worksheets and maybe your experience diary worksheet.

Battery charged: If you are using a mobile or portable phone, check the battery.

Call divert: Have your call divert set up to ensure that you are not getting incoming call bleeps in the middle of the interview.

Step 4. **Do the interview**

First impressions are important in a telephone interview. You create a good impression by:

- Sounding the part. Project confidence and enthusiasm for the job.

- Smiling while you are talking. While they will not see the smile, it will come through in your tone of voice.

- Writing the interviewers name on a sheet of paper so that you can refer to them by name.

- Speaking clearly.

USING THE TELEPHONE FOR JOB SEEKING

The telephone is a good way to look for a job or to find out about future opportunities. You can use the telephone to conduct research, cold call employers, make contacts and arrange to do interviews.

Using the telephone for job seeking requires skill and preparation. It is not like your average telephone conversation with a friend. The first thing is to be clear why you are ringing the employer in the first place.

Reasons for ringing an employer

1. **Get information** about the company, e.g. the name of the person who makes the hiring decisions, future vacancies etc.

2. **Speak to the person** who makes the hiring decisions (you should treat this conversation as a job interview – make a good impression).

3. **Be asked to an interview.**

4. **Get a job.**

While it is unlikely you will achieve all four objectives, every telephone call is an opportunity to get information.

Preparing to contact an employer about a job

The difference between a telephone job interview and using the telephone for job seeking is that you make the call. Before you make the call, you must think about what you are going to say, e.g. how you will introduce yourself, why are you ringing, what you want, etc.

Scripting

Scripting is when you plan what you intend to say before you make the call and avoid being tongue-tied during the call. We script all the time! If you have to talk about something important, make a speech, ask somebody out for a date etc., you plan what you are going to say in our mind first.

| **Exercise** | **Preparing your script** |

Write out your script on a blank page using the headings below. When you have finished, get a friend to act as an employer and do a practice telephone call with them.

BASIC DETAILS

Employer name and address, Tel. number, Contact name

The reasons for this call: List out what you want to achieve from this call.

SCRIPT – What are you going to say?

Introduction: Tell the person who you are.

Who am I speaking to? Get name of the person on the other end of the line. It makes the discussion more informal.

Opening statement: Why you are ringing.

List of questions to ask: List out questions you could ask to help get the information you need.

Possible negative responses: List possible negative responses and what you might say to overcome them.

REVIEW – What have you learned?

Results of telephone contact: Information obtained, good impression made, etc.

Any follow-up action to be taken: Send your CV, attend for interview, ring back, etc.

Lessons learned: How can I improve for the next telephone call?

PART 5

KEEPING YOUR JOB-SEEKING SKILLS UPDATED

CONTENTS

(i)   **The never-ending job hunt**

(ii) **Worksheet – My experience diary continuation sheet**

(iii) **How to succeed in the job after you've got it!**

THE NEVER-ENDING JOB HUNT

Your job-seeking activities do not just finish suddenly when you get a job. People move from job to job on an ongoing basis throughout their career. Even if you don't change employers, people change jobs in the same company through promotion, changes in company structures etc.

The basic principles of job seeking remain the same throughout your career – you must build up your skills, qualifications and experiences over time so that when a job opportunity comes up, you can convince the employer that you are a strong candidate for the job.

Keep your experience summary worksheets up to date

At this point, you will have completed all the experience summary and other job-seeking worksheets in this book. These worksheets will help you in your job-seeking activities as you go through your career. The only thing that changes is your experiences – these increase over time.

Remember that the employer is interested in your most recent experiences. With this in mind, keep your experience summary worksheets up to date and use them to update your CV on a continual basis.

You are as good as your last game

Employers are most interested in what you have done recently. Remember this when you are applying for a job in the future. Many job seekers tend to include everything in their CV or application. While this is fine early in your career, as your experiences increase it becomes harder to keep your information concise and your CV to a maximum of two pages.

How your CV changes over time

The content of your CV changes significantly over time. Today, education makes up a significant and important part of your CV. Once you start working full time, the work experience aspect becomes more and more important until it eventually dominates your CV.

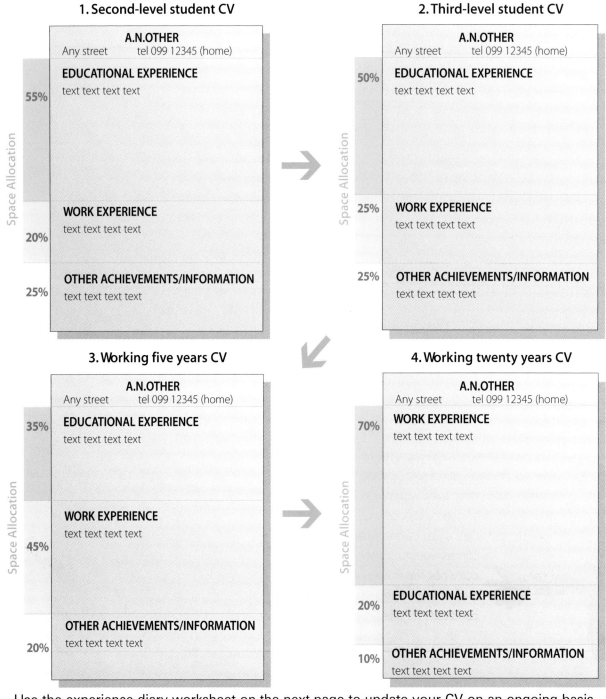

1. Second-level student CV

A.N.OTHER
Any street   tel 099 12345 (home)

EDUCATIONAL EXPERIENCE
text text text text

55%

WORK EXPERIENCE
text text text text

20%

OTHER ACHIEVEMENTS/INFORMATION
text text text text

25%

2. Third-level student CV

A.N.OTHER
Any street   tel 099 12345 (home)

50% **EDUCATIONAL EXPERIENCE**
text text text text

25% **WORK EXPERIENCE**
text text text text

25% **OTHER ACHIEVEMENTS/INFORMATION**
text text text text

3. Working five years CV

A.N.OTHER
Any street   tel 099 12345 (home)

35% **EDUCATIONAL EXPERIENCE**
text text text text

45% **WORK EXPERIENCE**
text text text text

20% **OTHER ACHIEVEMENTS/INFORMATION**
text text text text

4. Working twenty years CV

A.N.OTHER
Any street   tel 099 12345 (home)

70% **WORK EXPERIENCE**
text text text text

20% **EDUCATIONAL EXPERIENCE**
text text text text

10% **OTHER ACHIEVEMENTS/INFORMATION**
text text text text

Space Allocation

Use the experience diary worksheet on the next page to update your CV on an ongoing basis.

Worksheet | My Experience Diary Continuation Sheet

Use this worksheet to keep a record of new experiences and achievements. Use the summary worksheets on pages 13 to 16 to describe each activity in more detail in preparation for updating your CV/application, or preparing for an interview.

Year	Months	Brief Activity Description		
		Education	Work	Extra Curricular/Other
20_ _	July/Aug/Sept			
20_ _	Oct/Nov/Dec			
20_ _	Jan/Feb/Mar			
20_ _	April/May/June			
20_ _	July/Aug/Sept			
20_ _	Oct/Nov/Dec			
20_ _	Jan/Feb/Mar			
20_ _	April/May/June			

HOW TO SUCCEED IN THE JOB AFTER YOU'VE GOT IT!

JOB SUCCESS AHEAD

Once you've got a job, your next step is to be successful in it so that it acts as a basis for building up your skills and experiences for future job opportunities that may arise. There are basic things that you need to know and use to be successful at your job.

Guidelines for job success

Starting off

- Look and listen for the first few days to see what parts are most important. Talk to your manager or other staff about parts of the job you do not understand.

- Look at other people to see what are the good work practices in the company and apply those to your work.

- Find out the proper chain of command and whom you go to if there is a problem or you need to ask for help or advice.

- Be on time. How long will it take to get to work? Allow a few extra minutes for traffic problems, etc. A good timekeeper gains the trust and respect of an employer.

- Be patient, it takes time to learn a new job. It is useful, however, to set a date in your mind by which you want to be on top of the job.

- Find out and follow the office rules, policies and procedures.

On the Job

- A positive attitude is one of the most important things in job success.

- Be friendly and helpful to people.

- Have a good attendance record. If you are sick, let the employer know as soon as possible.

- Listen and learn. Be open to new ways of doing things and be willing and enthusiastic about learning new skills.

- Don't be a 'know all'. Be slow to find fault, criticise or complain until you are sure that you can do something a better way.

- If you need to talk with your supervisor, ask them if they can talk now or when would be a good time to meet.

- Wear clean and job-appropriate clothes. See what other workers wear.

- Don't use the employer's equipment and time to do personal things like making personal phone calls, using the photocopier, surf the Web, send personal emails or text messages, etc. Switch off your mobile phone.

- If you need help, ask and learn. If you make a mistake, let your supervisor know immediately and find out how you can fix it. Do not make the same mistake or ask the same question twice.

Personal development

- Find a mentor, someone who you respect and knows the employer and the job well enough to coach you and show you the ropes.

- Criticism from a manager or supervisor can be constructive. Don't be defensive or take it personally. Think about the criticism and discuss it further if you feel it is unwarranted or do not understand it. If the criticism is correct – change and learn from the experience.

- Take time in making new friends. Find positive co-workers, avoid negative, critical or gossiping people.

- If the employer conducts performance reviews, use them to your advantage to get extra training, increase wages, and find out areas in which you could improve your skills.

- Be a team player. Know what is expected of you and how your job fits into the team's activities.